Tassos Katsikas

The Greek Armored Cruiser Georgios Averof 1911-1913

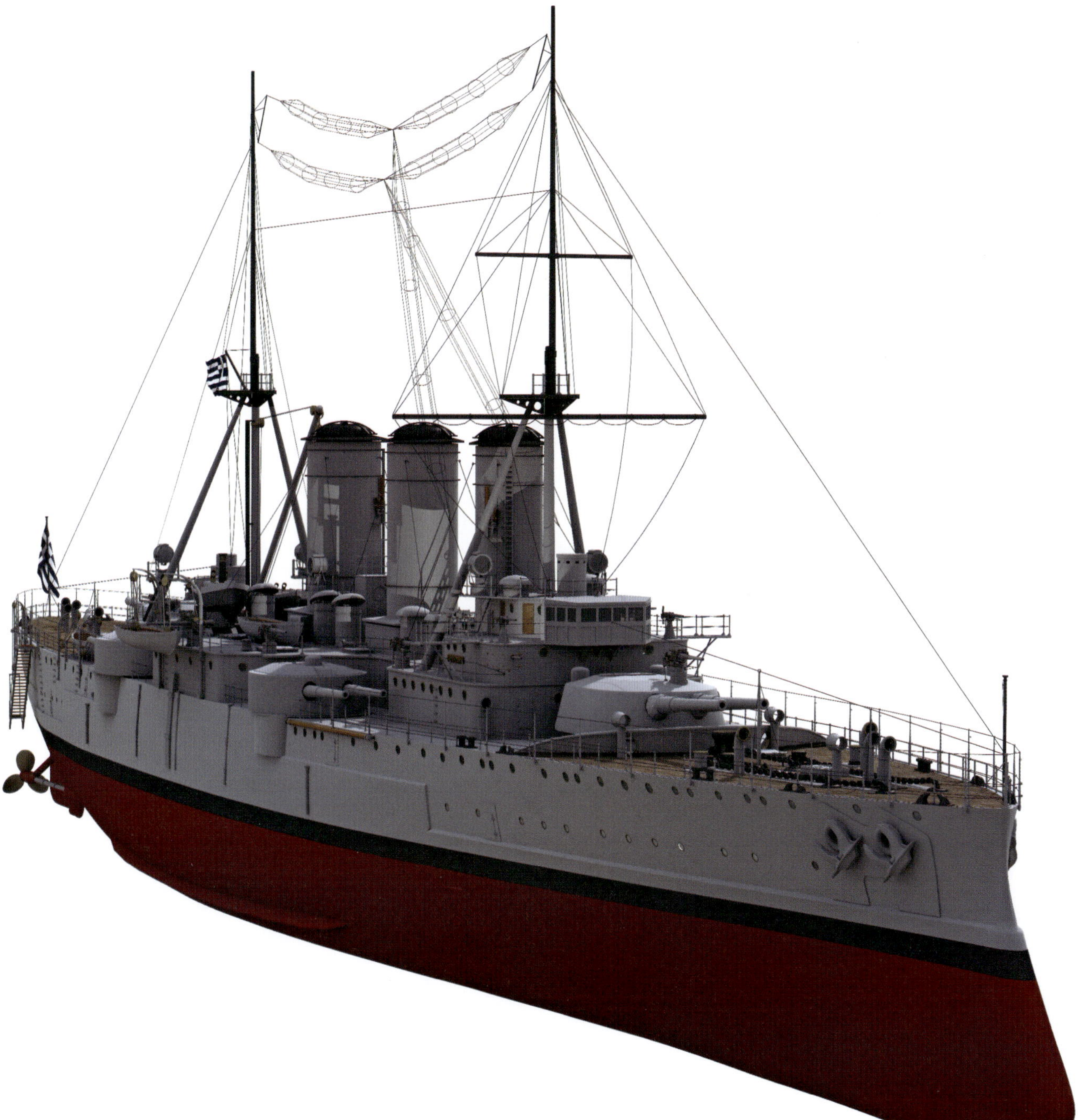

KAGERO

Starboard side view.

Overview

Georgios Averof (Θ/Κ Γεώργιος Αβέρωφ) is a *Pisa* class armored cruiser of the pre-dreadnought era. The ship was the third from the series of *Pisa* class ships after *Pisa* and *Amalfi*. The ship initially (1907) was ordered for *Marinha do Brasil*, but one year later the Brazilian government abandoned the order. As a result of this decision, the construction works for the armored cruiser halted. However in 1909 the ship was acquired by the *Royal Hellenic Navy* and named *Georgios Averof*. The new ship took his name from the Greek benefactor *Georgios Averof* who died in Egypt in 1899. *Georgios Averof* left in his will an enormous amount of money for the purchase of an educational ship for the needs of the Greek navy young cadets. Under the circumstances, the Hellenic Government decided to use the money of *G. Averof's* inheritance for the armored cruiser. Thus the Greek Government paid to Orlando shipyards £250,000 in gold, or one quarter of the purchase price. The decision for this purchase was not an easy task for the Greek government for two main reasons. First, the price of the ship was particularly high for a poor state such as Greece, while the Greek government had to overcome the obstacle of King George I who was a relative of Kaiser. The Germans obviously wanted to sell a German warship instead of an Italian, French or British, in order to increase their political influence in the Greek state. The ship was launched in 1910 (12 March) and completed 14 months later (16 May 1911). She served as the flagship of the Hellenic Navy from 1911 to 1952 and participated in the Balkan wars of 1912-1913 against the Ottoman navy in the crucial battles of Elli and Lemnos. Moreover, *Averof* participated in the victorious campaigns of North and Central Aegean Islands, as well as in the campaigns for the liberation of the coastal cities of East Macedonia and Thrace. The ship played a minor role in the WWI mainly because of the neutrality of the Greek government in the first years. In the end of WWI she sailed in Constatinople and raised the Hellenic flag as Greece was one of the winning powers. Due to these operations, the ship gained a dominant position as a symbol of national pride. She also participated actively in the Greco-Turkish war of 1919-1922 and helped in the evacuation of the Greek troops and refugees from Asia Minor. In WWII the ship escaped to Alexandria after the German invasion of 1941, and moved to Red Sea and Indian Ocean acting as an escort ship for convoys. After the withdrawal of the Germans from Greece in 1944, she carried back the exiled Greek government to the port of Piraeus from Middle East. The last voyage of the ship was in Rhodes in May of 1945 during the preparations for the annexation of the Dodecanese islands to Greece. In 1945 the ship operated as fleet headquarters and finally decommissioned in 1952. *Georgios Aversof* is the only survived armored cruiser in the world. Today is operating as a museum ship in Naval Museum Park in Faliro, Greece. In 2017 the ship with the help of a fleet of tugs was towed from Athens to Thessaloniki and vise-versa. During his 50 day stay in the port of Thessaloniki the ship was visited by more than 130.000 citizens.

Design

The end of the 19th century was accompanied by an armament race between England and Germany for the control of the sea routes. The ideal battleship had to be light weight in order to achieve maximum speed, but with enough armor and big guns. The Italian shipyards tried to followed the British and German shipyards and designed effective and fast - enough armored cruisers capable of successfully dealing with heavier and stronger warships. The 7350 tons *Cusieppe Garibaldi* class armored cruiser was a typical example. This design approach attracted as customers smaller sea powers like Argentina, Spain, Japan with limited resources in order to purchase conventional battleships for their fleet. Argentina bought 4 ships (*Garibaldi, San Martin, Belgrano, Puetrredóm*), Spain bought one (*Cristóbal Colón*) and Japan bought 2 ships (*Kasuga* and *Nisshin*). In 1901 Italians presented the *Regina-Elena* class a 13.800 tons class battleship designed by the naval engineer *Vittorio Cuniberti* a visionary ship

designer. *Cuniberti's* article of 1903 *"An ideal battleship for the British fleet"* was the cornerstone for the British Dreadnought class battleship. The Italians tried to repeat the success of the Garibaldi class by presenting the *Pisa* class armored cruiser. The *Pisa* class armored cruiser was an attempt to replicate in a smaller scale the armament and the armor of the *Regina-Elena* battleships. The ship was designed in 1905 by the Italian engineer *Guiseppe Orlando* and the shipbuilding started in the *Cantiere Navale Fratelli Orlando* shipyard in Livorno. The Italian navy ordered two units under the names *Pisa* and Amalfi. *Pisa* class ships had a length of 140.13 meters (459 ft 8in.), beam 21 meters (68 ft 11 in.) and draught of 7.1 meters (23 ft 4 in.). Their displacement was 9,956 long tons (10,116 metric tons) at normal load and 10,600 long tons (10,770 metric tons) at deep load, while their complement was 30 officers and 670 enlisted men.

Ships

Name	Builder	Laid down	Launched	Completed	Fate
Pisa	Orlando, Livorno	20 February 1905	15 September 1907	1 September 1909	Discarded, 28 April 1937
Amalfi	Odero,Genoa--Sestri Ponente	24July 1905	5 May 1908	1September 1909	Sunk, 7 July 1915
Georgios Averof	Orlando, Livorno	1907	12March 1910	16May 1911	Training, accomodation ship, Poros Island, 1952-1983 Museum ship, 1984

Propulsion

Averof was powered by two vertical four-cylinder triple-expansion reciprocating engines of the Italian firm *Gio Ansaldo & C.* Each engine was

General characteristics

Name:	*Georgios Averof* (Θ/Κ Γεώργιος Αβέρωφ)
Class and type:	*Pisa*-class armored cruiser
Builder:	Cantiere Navale Fratelli Otlando, Livorno
Launched:	12 March 1910
Commissioned:	16 May 1911
Decommissioned:	1 August 1952
Status:	Museum ship
Displacement:	9,956 long tons (10,116 t) Standard
Length:	140.13 m (459 ft 8 in.)
Beam:	21 m (68 ft 11 in.)
Draft:	7.1 m (23 ft 4in.)
Propulsion:	2 × compound-expansion Ansaldo steam engines, 2 × shafts
Power:	22 x Belleville Boilers ,19.000 shp (14.000 kW)
Speed:	23.5 knots (43.5 km/h; 27.0 mph) maximum
	20 knots (37 km/h; 23 mph) operational
Range:	8,416 nmi (15,576 km; 9,672 mi) at 14 knots
	2,480 nmi (4,590 km; 2,850 mi) at 17.5 knots
	1400 nmi (2,593 km; 1,611 mi) at 22,5 knots
Fuel:	660 tons (up to 1542 tons)
Armament:	**Original configuration (1911)**
	2x twin 234 mm (9.2 in) guns
	4xtwin 190mm (7.5 in) guns
	16x 76mm (3 in) guns
	4x37mm (1.85 in) guns
	3x457mm (18 in) torpedo tubes
	After refit (1925-1927)
	2x twin 234 mm (9.2 in) guns
	4xtwin 190mm (7.5 in) guns
	8x 76mm (3 in) guns
	4x 76mm (3 in) AA guns
	4x37mm (1.85 in) guns
	3x430mm (17 in) torpedo tubes
	6 × single 36 mm (1.42 in) AA guns
Armor:	Main belt: 200 mm (7.9 in) at midship; 80 mm (3.15 in) at ends
	Deck: 40 mm (1.6 in)
	Turrets: 200 mm (7.9 in) at 234mm turrets; 175 mm (6.9 in) at 190mm turrets
	Barbettes: 180 mm (7.1 in)
	Conning tower: 170 mm (7.1 in)
Complement:	30 officers and 670 men (max 1200)

Port side view.

driving one propeller and both engines were supported by twenty-two French-made *Belleville* water-tube type boilers. The boilers were divided in four rooms in order to minimize possible damages from enemy hits. The engines were designed in order to deliver a full power of 19,000 shp, while in extreme cases could deliver a power of 21,500 shp. The speed of the ship was 22.5 knots (41.7km/h; 25.9 mph). However both *Averof* and *Pisa/Amalfi* reached the speed of 23.6 knots (43.7 km/h; 27.1 mph) during sea trials. The bunker capacity of the ship was 660 tons of coal in the ordinary way, while in extreme conditions the capacity could reach 1,500 tons thus allowing a cruising range of 2,500 nautical miles (4,600 km; 2,900 mi) with an average speed of 12 knots (22 km/h; 14mph). At full speed the range was reduced to 1400 nautical miles (2,600 km; 1,600 mi).

Armament

The essential difference between G. *Averof* and the two Italian *Pisa*-class ships was their main armament. The main armament for the Italian ships consisted of four 254mm (10.0 in) Italian guns (Cannone da 254/45 V Modello 1906). The Royal Hellenic Navy selected the Armstrong Mark X 234mm (9.2 in) guns. These guns guns could launch a shell of 172kg (380 pounds) with a muzzle velocity of 840 m/s (2,770ft/s), propelled by an explosive 46.7kg (103lb). As their secondary armament the Italian ships were fitted with eight 190mm (7.5 in) guns (Cannone da 190/45 V Modello 1906) in four hydraulic double-gun turrets, two on each side in the middle of the ship. On the contrary, *Averof* was equipped with eight guns 190mm (7.5 in) from Armstrong. These guns could launch a shell of 90kg (200lb) shell fired by a 21.3kg (47lb) charge to a muzzle velocity of 792m/s (2,600ft/s). The turrets and the size of the guns followed the design standards of the typical armoured cruiser of 1910. The main guns could be rotated to fire in three directions, forward, port and starboard. The turrets were rotated hydraulically on the barbettes, while the guns could be turned manually in an emergency situation. One of the more remarkable features of the *Averof* was

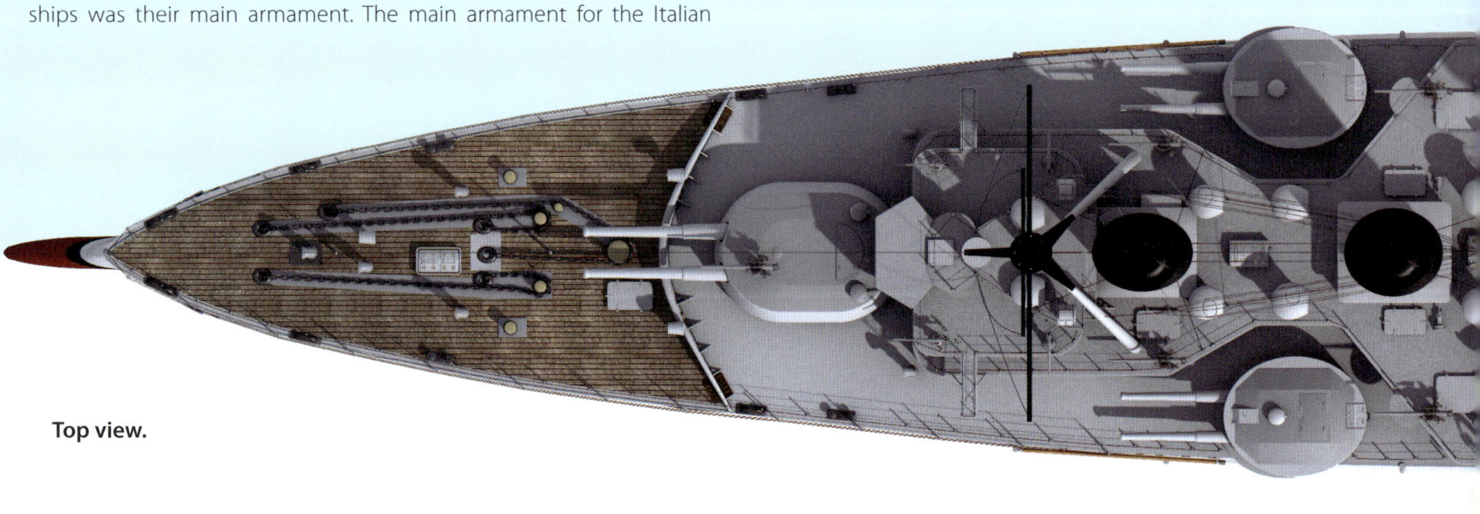

Top view.

its firecontrol system with optical rangefinders was located far enough from the tree chimneys and was practically independent from the coal smoke. For defense against torpedo boats all three ships were fitted with 16 Vickers QF 76mm(3in) guns. *Averof* was equipped with four 37mm QF guns, while the Italian ones with 8 47mm guns. The two Italian ships were equipped with three submerged 450 mm (17.7 in) torpedo tubes while those of Georgios Averof were 457 mm (18.0 in) one at the stern and two on either side below the bridge.

Protection

The ship was well protected, according to the 1910 military protection standards with steel supplied by the Italian company SAFFAT(Terni). The hull was protected by an armored belt that was 200 mm (7.9 in) thick amidships and reduced to 90 mm (3.5 in) at the bow and stern. The 254 mm gun turrets were protected by 160mm (6.3 in) of steel, while the 190mm gun turrets had an armored belt of 140mm (5.51in) steel. The fire control system and the combat bridge were protected by an armored belt of 180 mm (7.75 in) capable of absorbing a direct hit from a 234 mm (9.2in) gun. The conning tower armor was 180mm (7.1 in) thick and the armored deck was protected with a 51mm (2.0 in) steel protection. As ship of Italian origin, *Averof* followed the standard ship design, as his double bottom was divided into eighteen watertight compartments for sinking protection.

Career

The ship participated in the Coronation Fleet Review for King George V of England in 1911 shortly after commissioning. With the outbreak of the Balkan Wars in October 1912, *Averof* served as the flagship of the Hellenic fleet, and she took part in the takeover of the islands of the northern and eastern Aegean. *Averof* was the most modern anf

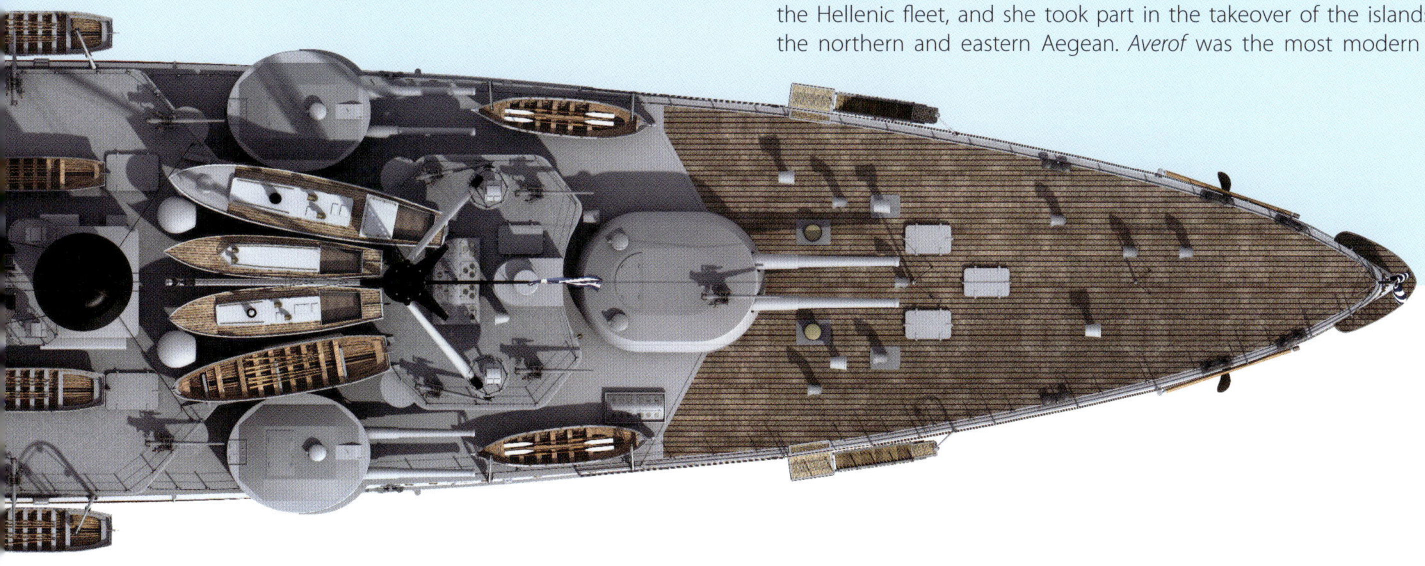

powerfull ship of the Balkan League (Greece, Bulgaria, Serbia and Montenegro) against the Ottoman Turks. She participated in the naval battles of Elli (3 December 1912) and Lemnos (5 January 1913) against the Ottoman navy. The ship almost alone secured victory and the undisputed control of the Aegean Sea for Greece. *Averof* in both battles pursued the Turkish fleet alone as she was superior in speed, armor and armament. During the Battle of Elli, Admiral *Pavlos Kountouriotis* raised the flag for the letter Z, which meant "Independent Action" and proceeded alone at a speed of 20 knots (37 km/h) against the Turkish fleet. *Averof* succeeded in crossing the T of the Turkish fleet and gathered her fires against the Ottoman flagship (*Hayreddin Barbarossa*), forcing the Ottoman fleet to retreat in Dardanelles Strait. Similarly, one month later during the Battle of Lemnos, *Kountouriotis* did not hesitate to pursue the Ottoman fleet again. In both battles the ship suffered minor damages while caused serious damage to several Turkish ships. After the Battle of Lemnos Averof nicknamed as "*Lucky Uncle George*". The ship is also credited for the closing of the Aegean sea to Ottoman military transports during the first Balkan War.

The neutrality of Greece in the first Years of WWI was the main reason for the minor role of the ship in WWI The ship played a minor role in the WWI mainly because of the neutrality of the Greek government in the first years. After the riots of November 1916, the ship was seized by France until 1917 when Greece joined the Entente. In the end of WWI she sailed in Constatinople and raised the Hellenic flag as Greece was one of the winning powers. Between 1919-1922 the ship participated in the Greco-Turkish war and supported troop landings in Earstern Thrace, participated in the bombardment of the Turkish Black Sea coastline, and in the end of the war helped in the evacuation of the Greek troops and refugees from Asia Minor. Between 1925-1927 the ship faced a major refit in Toulon, France. Al of the Bellevile water tube boilers were replaced, the torpedo tubes closed, new cranes added, while some of the lighter guns were replaced by anti-aircraft guns. Finally, a new and more strong foremast was placed. On the top of the new foremast an enhanced (with optical finders) fire control system was placed. One more time (after 1911), *Averof* participated at the 1935 Silver Jubilee Fleet Review for King

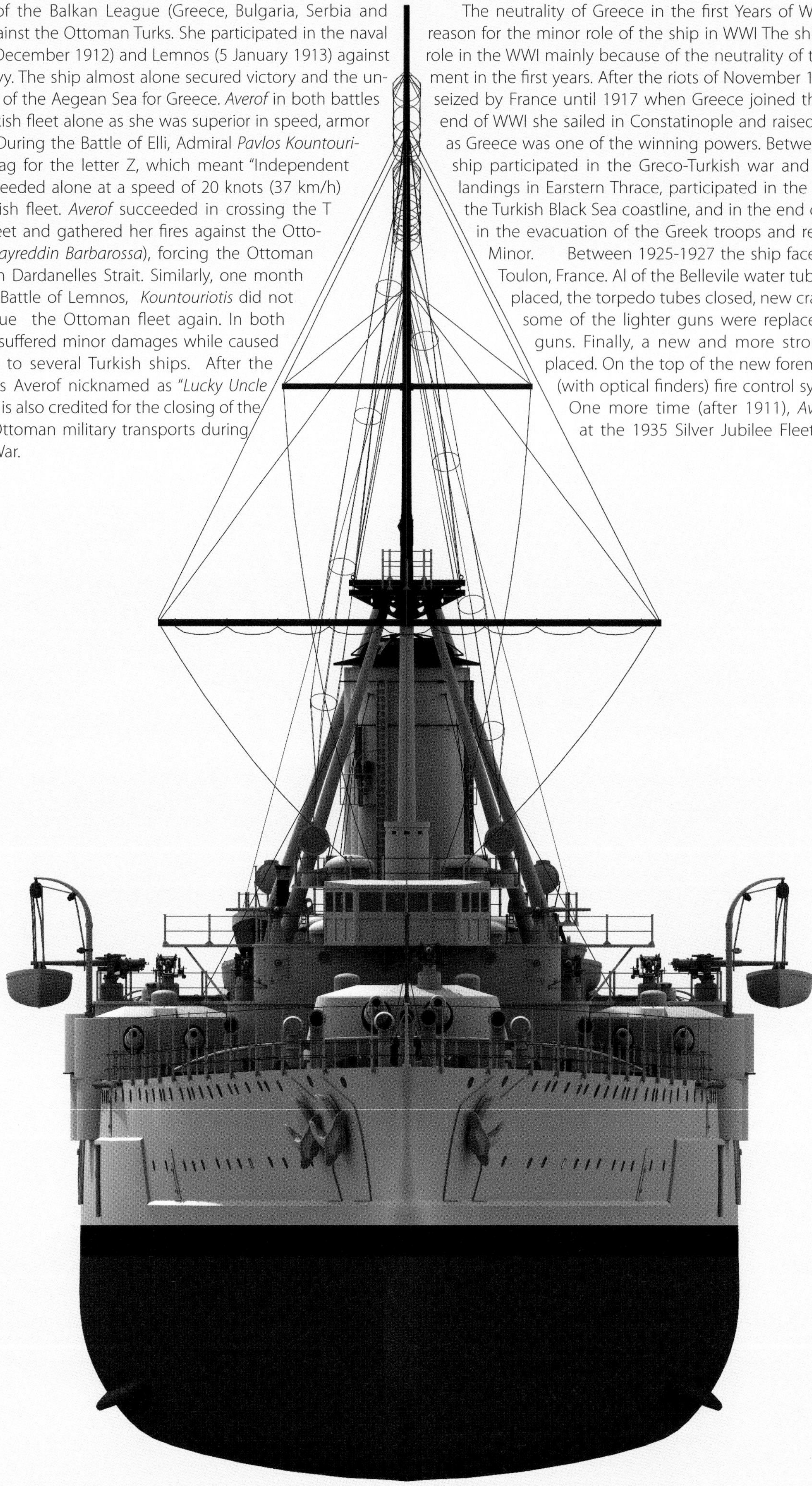

Bow view.

George V and she was the only ship which had also attended the previous coronation review in 1911. In WWII *Averof* was already an old ship and she managed to escape to Egypt after the German invasion of April 1941 in Greece. Initially the ship moved to the island of Crete in Souda Bay, and then to Alexandria, Egypt. The ship's limited armor and firepower (compared to modern battleships) as well as the obsolete coal fueling engine system forced *Averof* to withdraw from the Mediteranean sea and to move to the Indian Ocean. From September of 1941 through October 1942, she was assigned to convoy escort and patrol duties in the Indian Ocean and based at Bombay. After Bombay the old ship returned to the Port Said and in Lebanon. On 17 October 1944, *Averof* as the flagship of the exiled Hellenic Navy returned to the port of Piraeus, under the command of Captain *Theodoros Kountouriotis* (Admiral's son). The ship carried the Greek government-in-exile from Cairo to Athens. One day later, *Averof's* big flag was raised again in Acropolis. After 1945 she served as fleet headquarters and decommissioned in 1952. In 1984 the Hellenic Navy decided to restore *G. Averof* as a museum ship. The ship in the same year was towed to Palaio Faliro, Athens.

On 26 April 2017, *Averof* was towed from her museum dock to the Skaramangas Shipyard, in Elefsis where she spent two months for dry dock inspection and hull maintenance. In 5 October 2017, the ship towed to the port of Thesalloniki for a 50 day visit, as she returned back to Palaio Faliro in 13 December 2017. Today the ship (the only survived armored cruiser worldwide) is anchored as functioning floating museum, promoting the Greek naval tradition.

Bibliography

Carr John, *RHNS Averof, Thunder in the Aegean, London*, Pen & Sword Maritime, 2014

Fotakis, Zhshs. *Greek Naval Strategy and Policy 1910–1919*, London and New York, Routledge 2005

Arnold-Baker, R. and Cremos, G, *Averof: The Ship That Changed The Course Of History*, Athens: Akritas Publications 1990

Stern view.

View of ships hull and superstructures from starboard side.

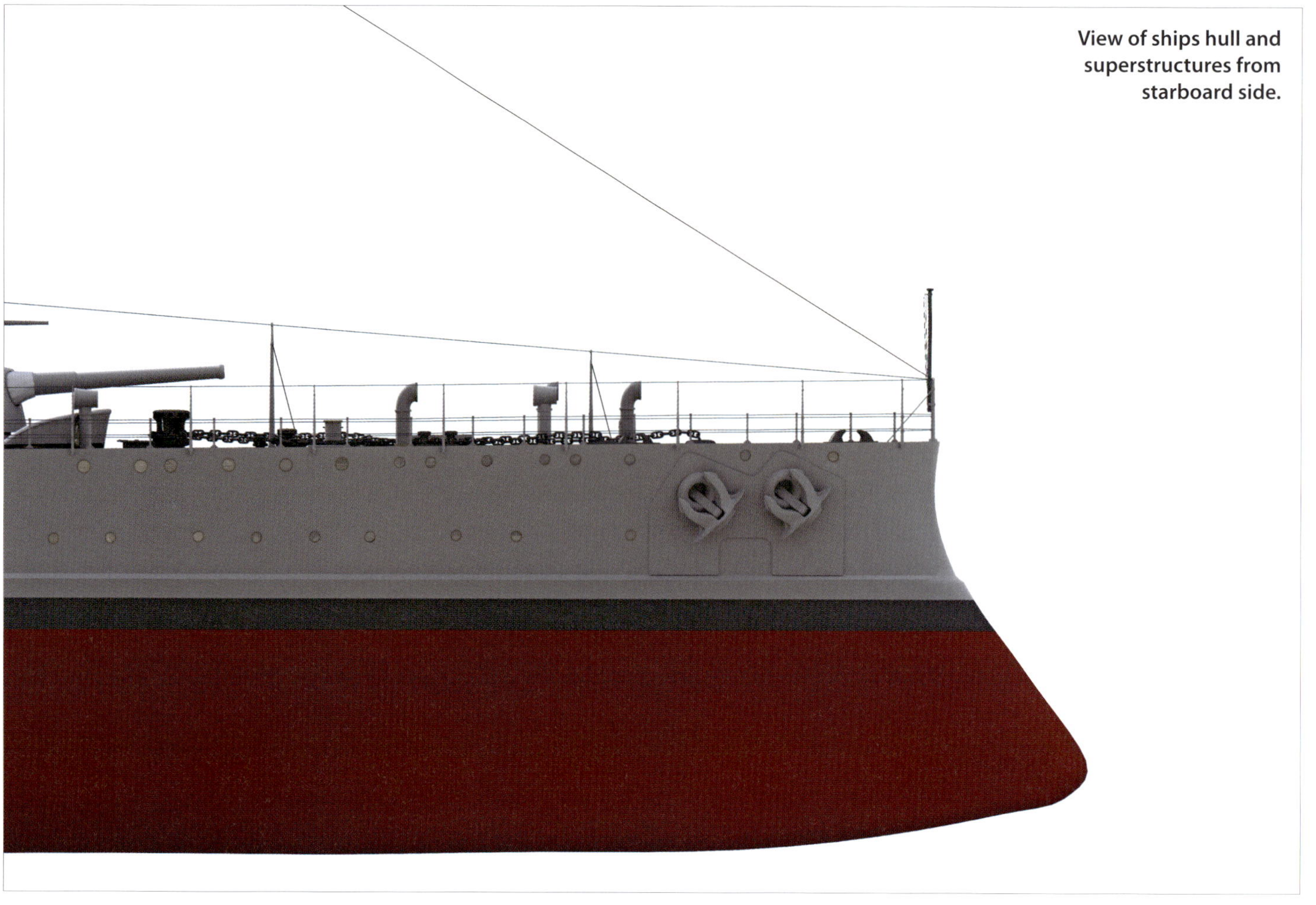

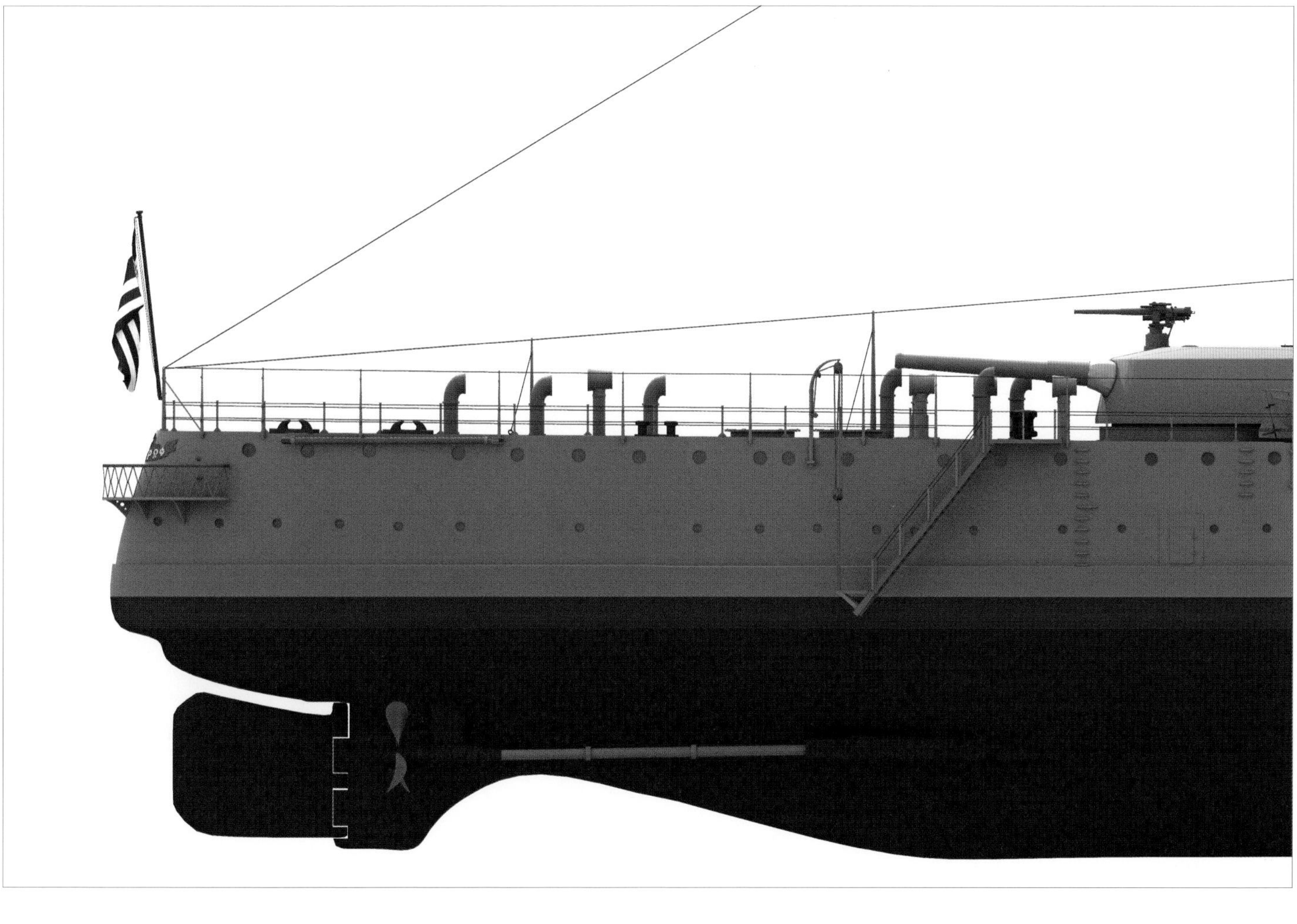

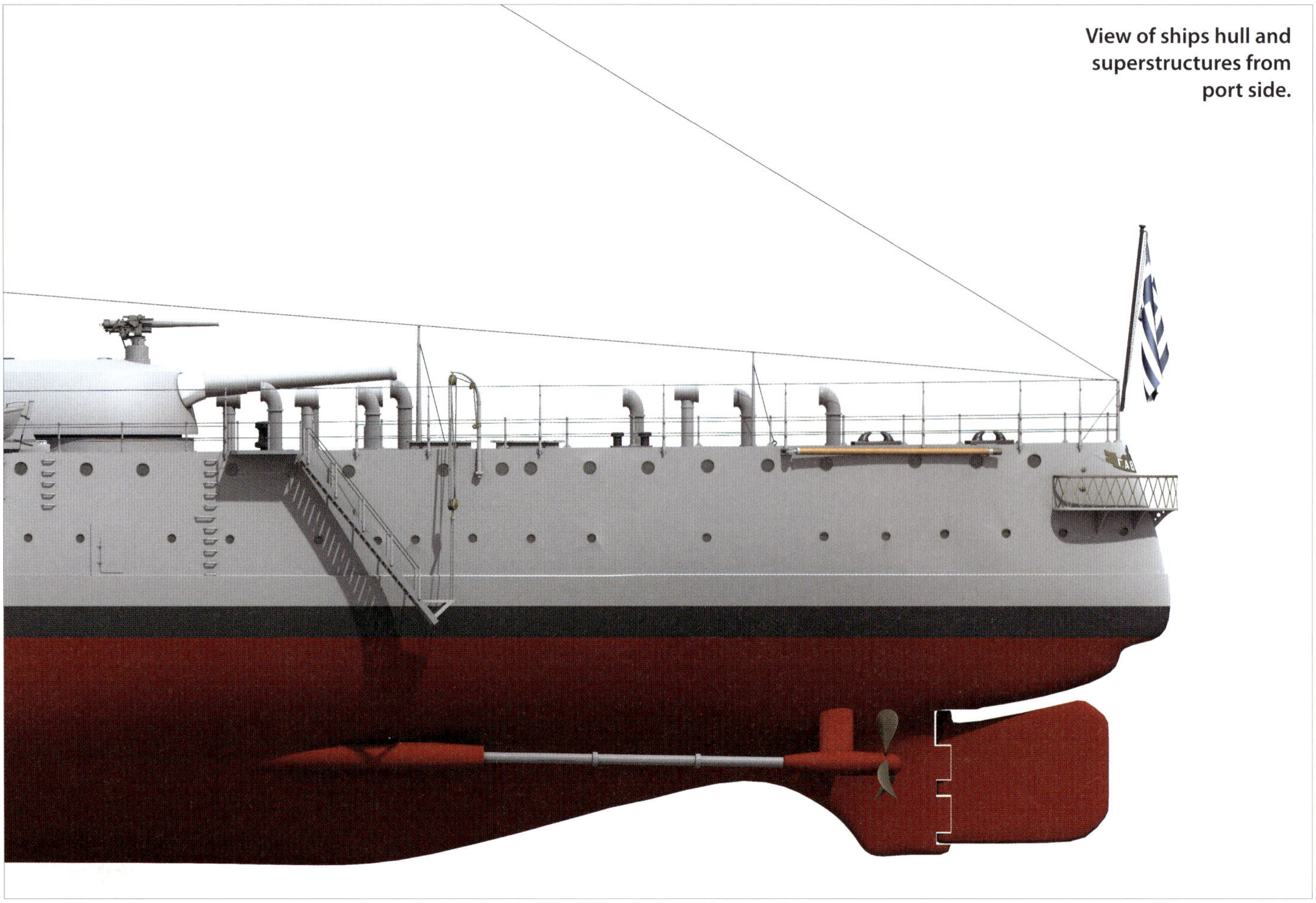

View of ships hull and superstructures from port side.

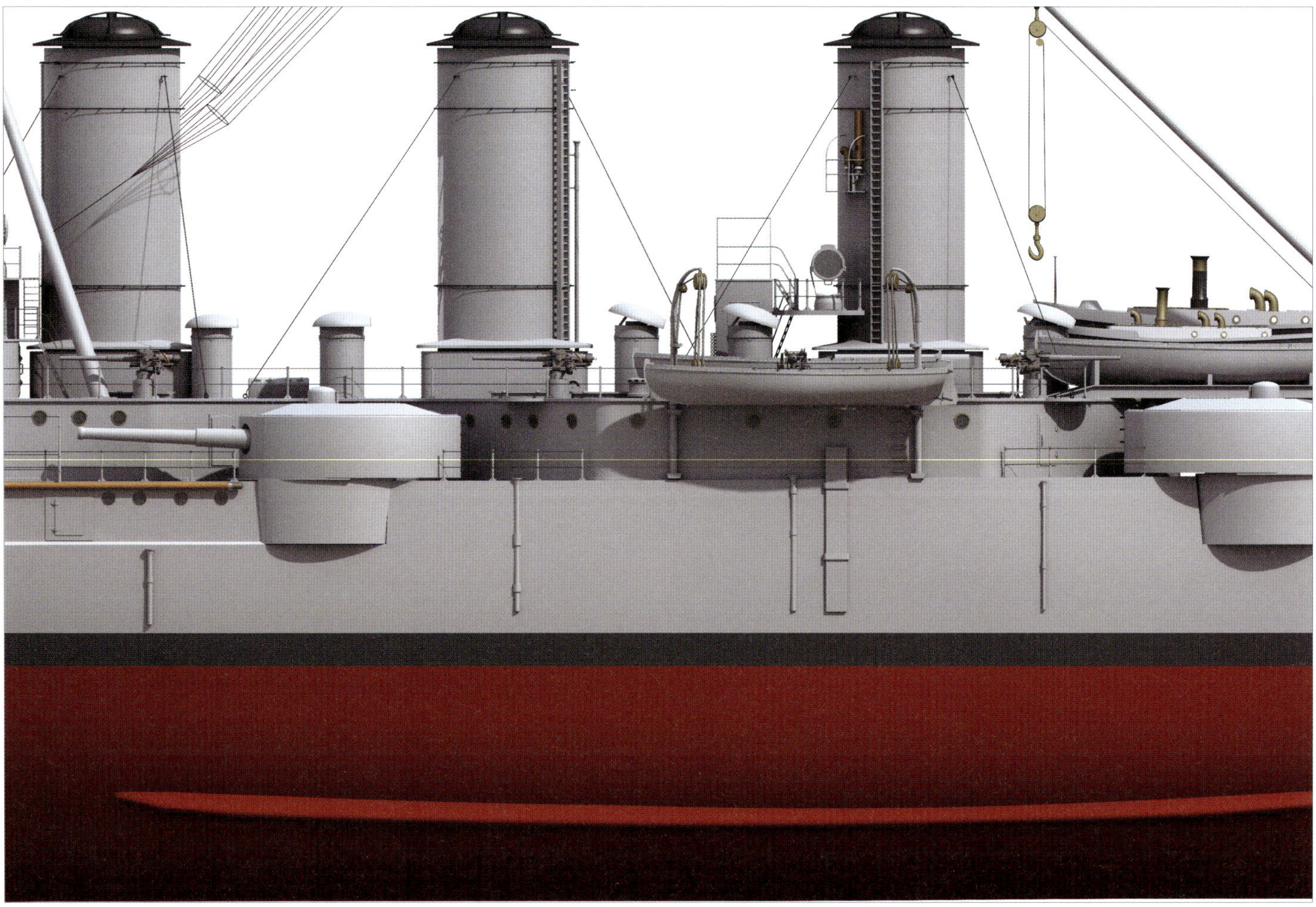

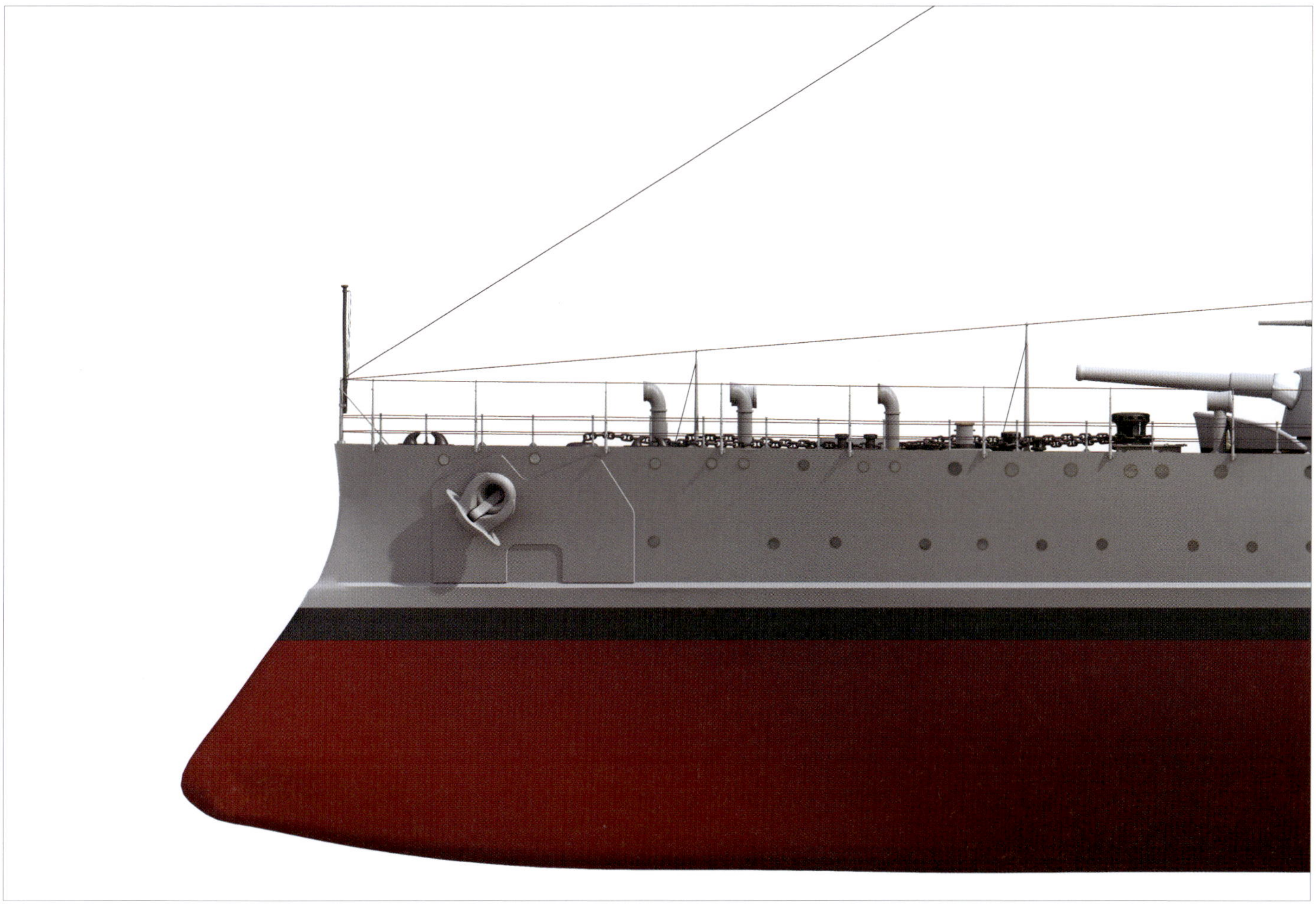

View of ships hull and superstructures from top

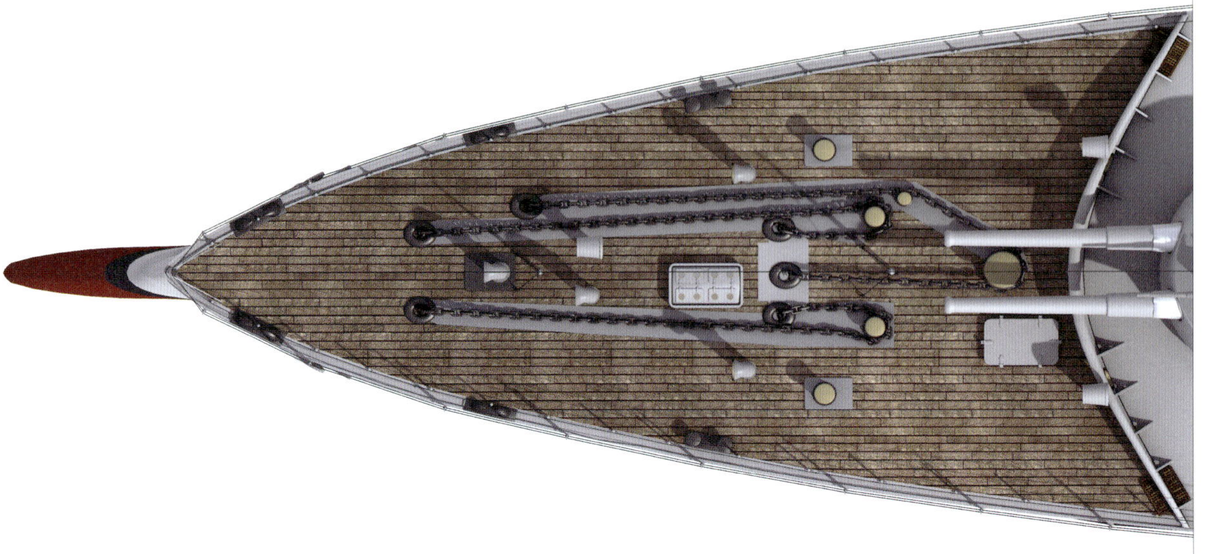

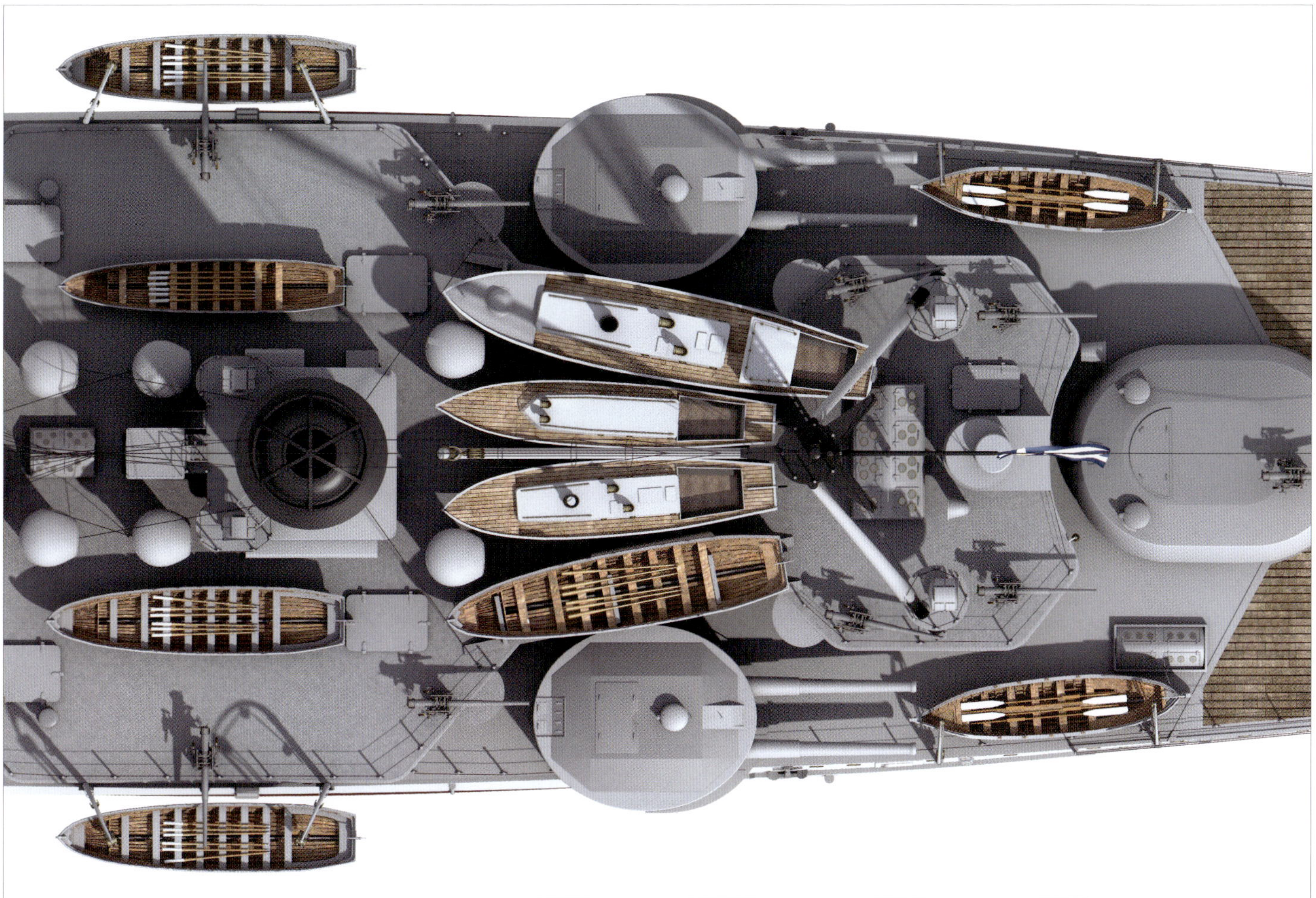

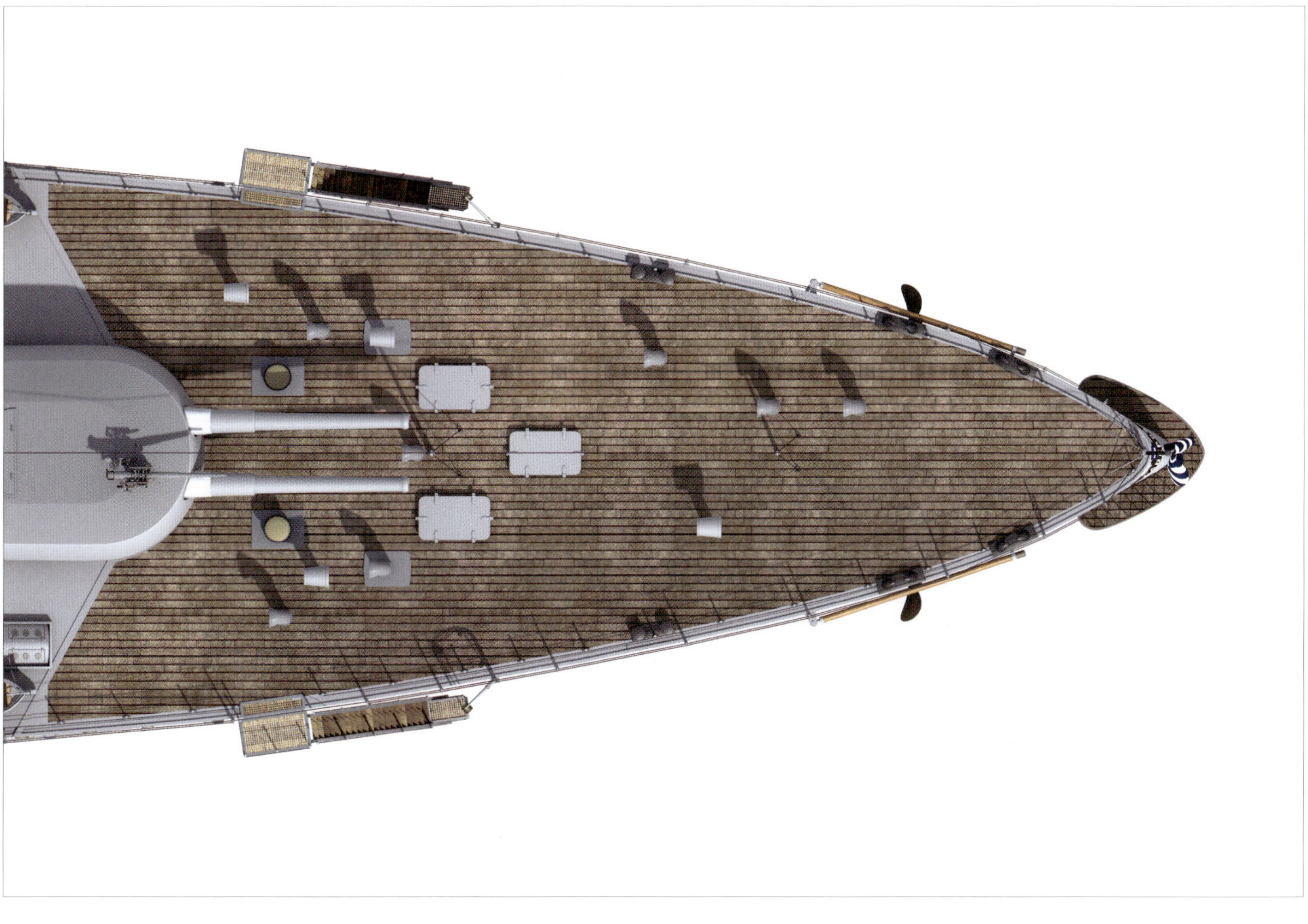

Overall view of the bow.

Overall view of the front 234 mm armoured turret.

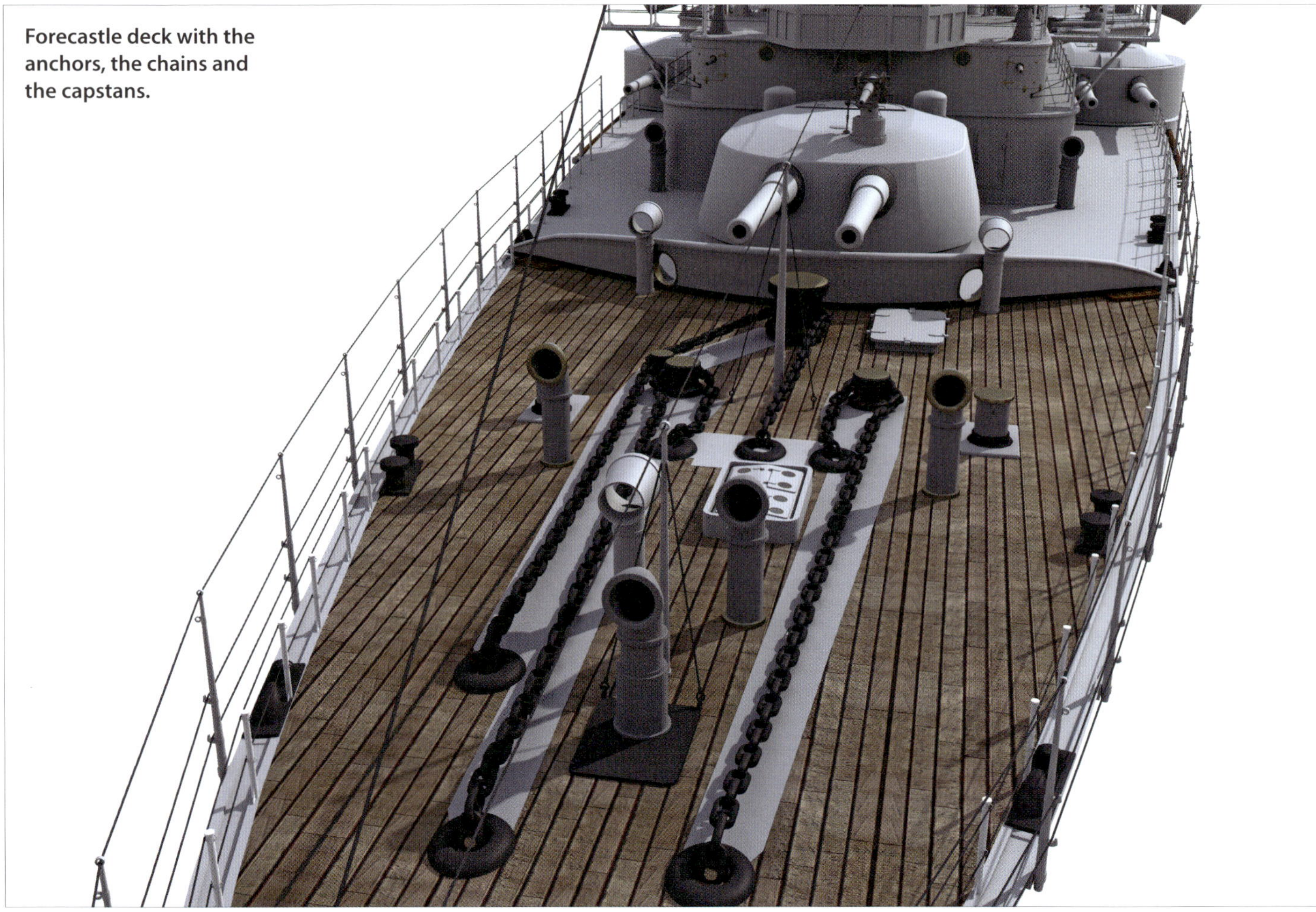

Forecastle deck with the anchors, the chains and the capstans.

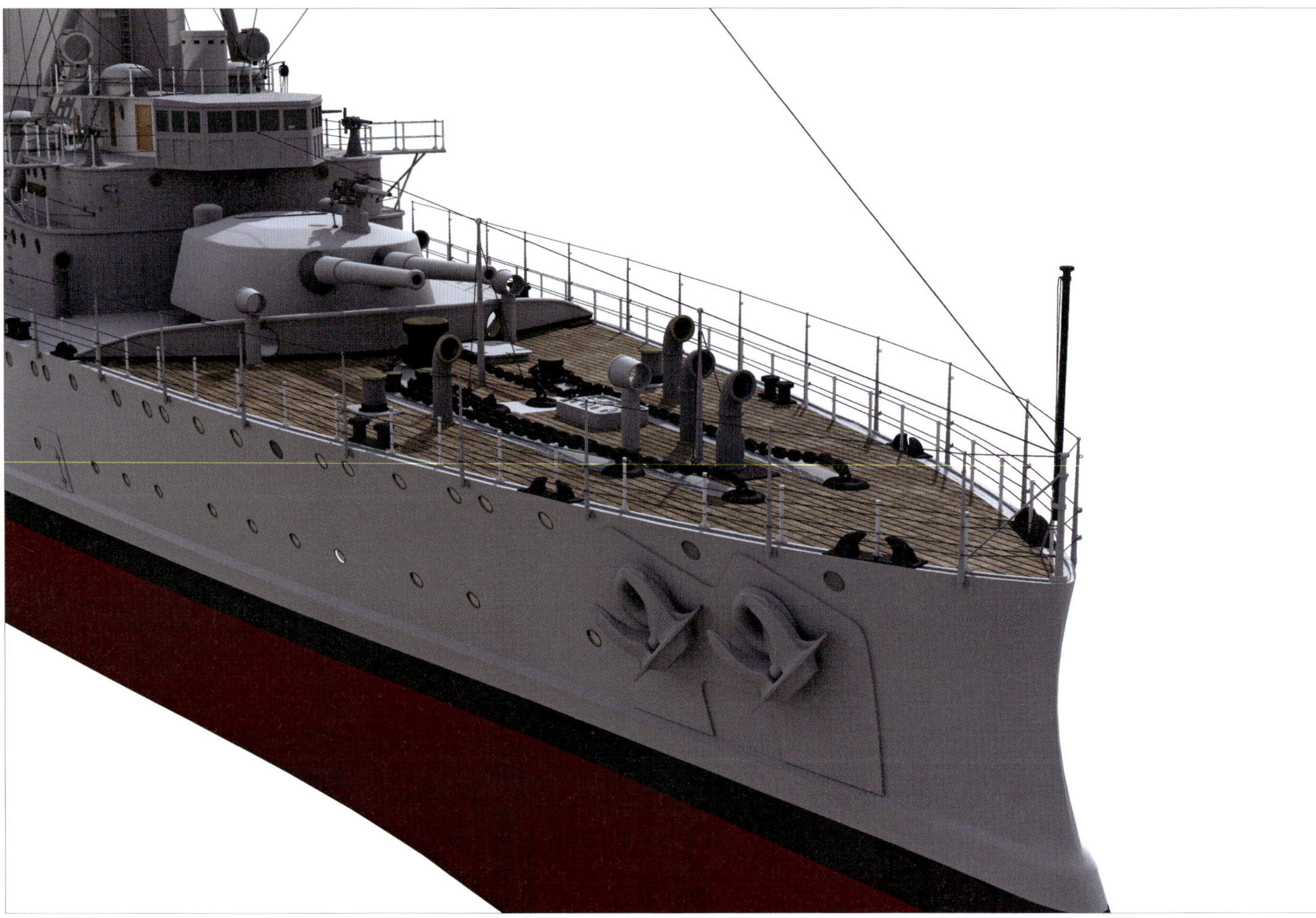

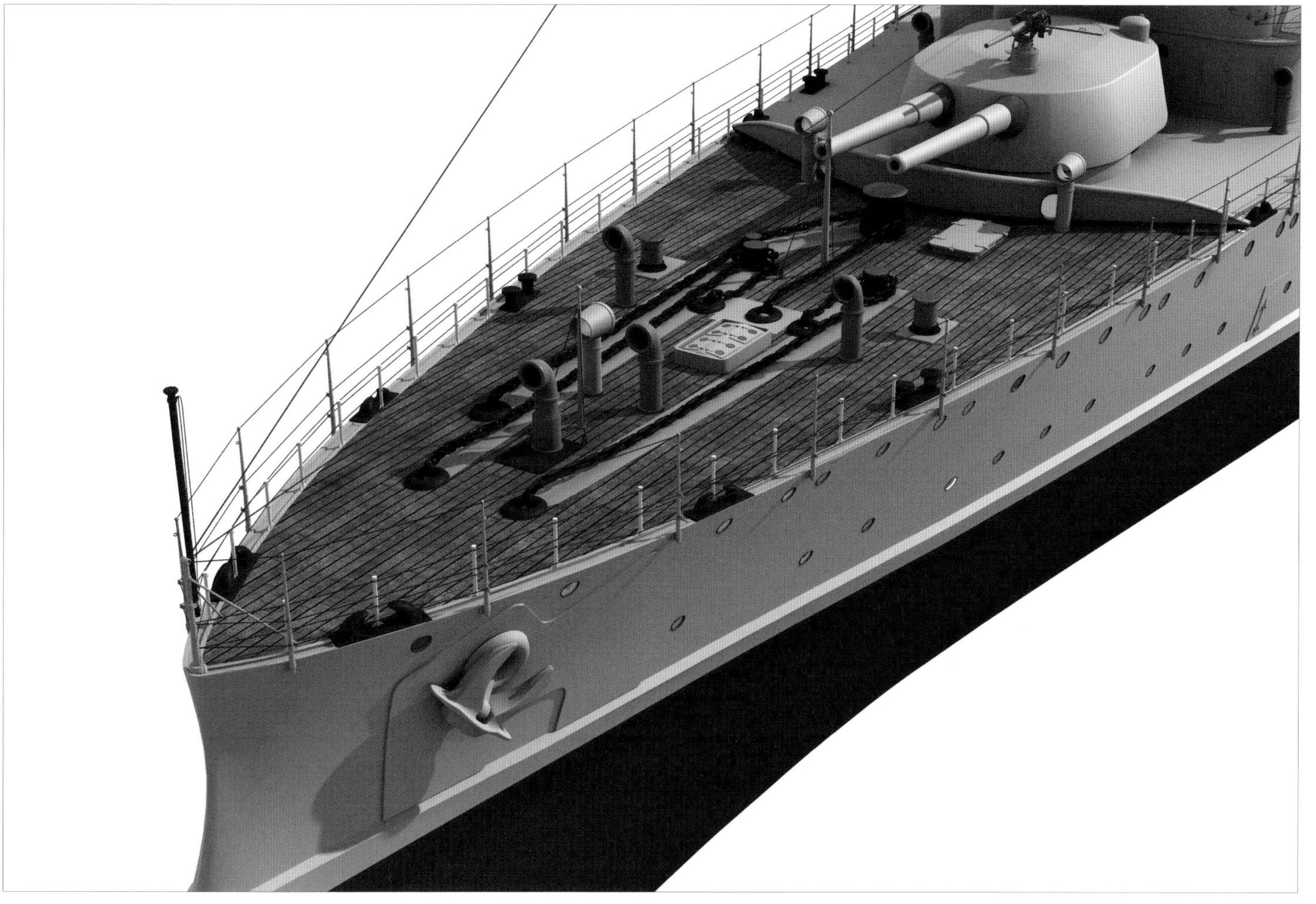

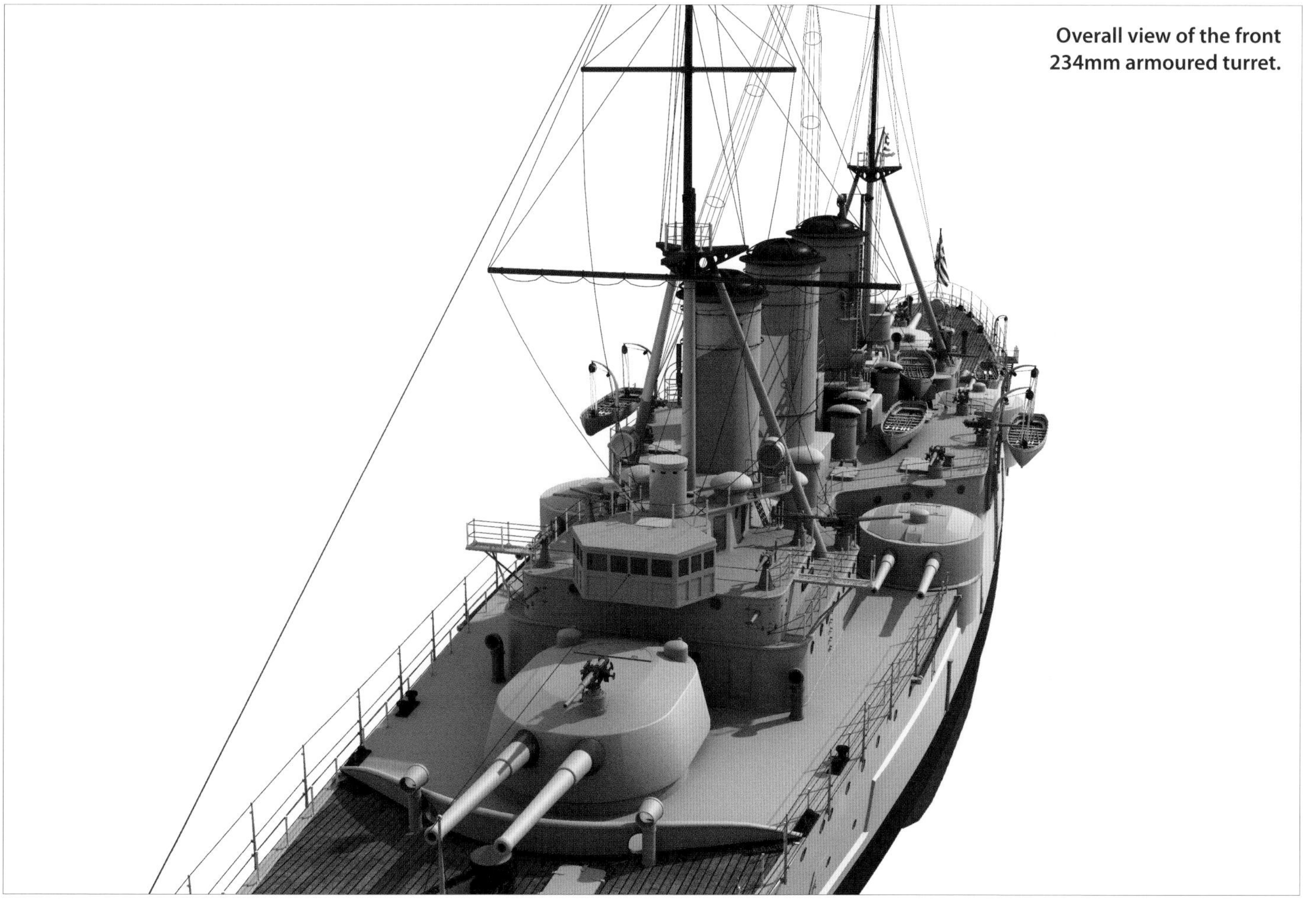

Overall view of the front 234mm armoured turret.

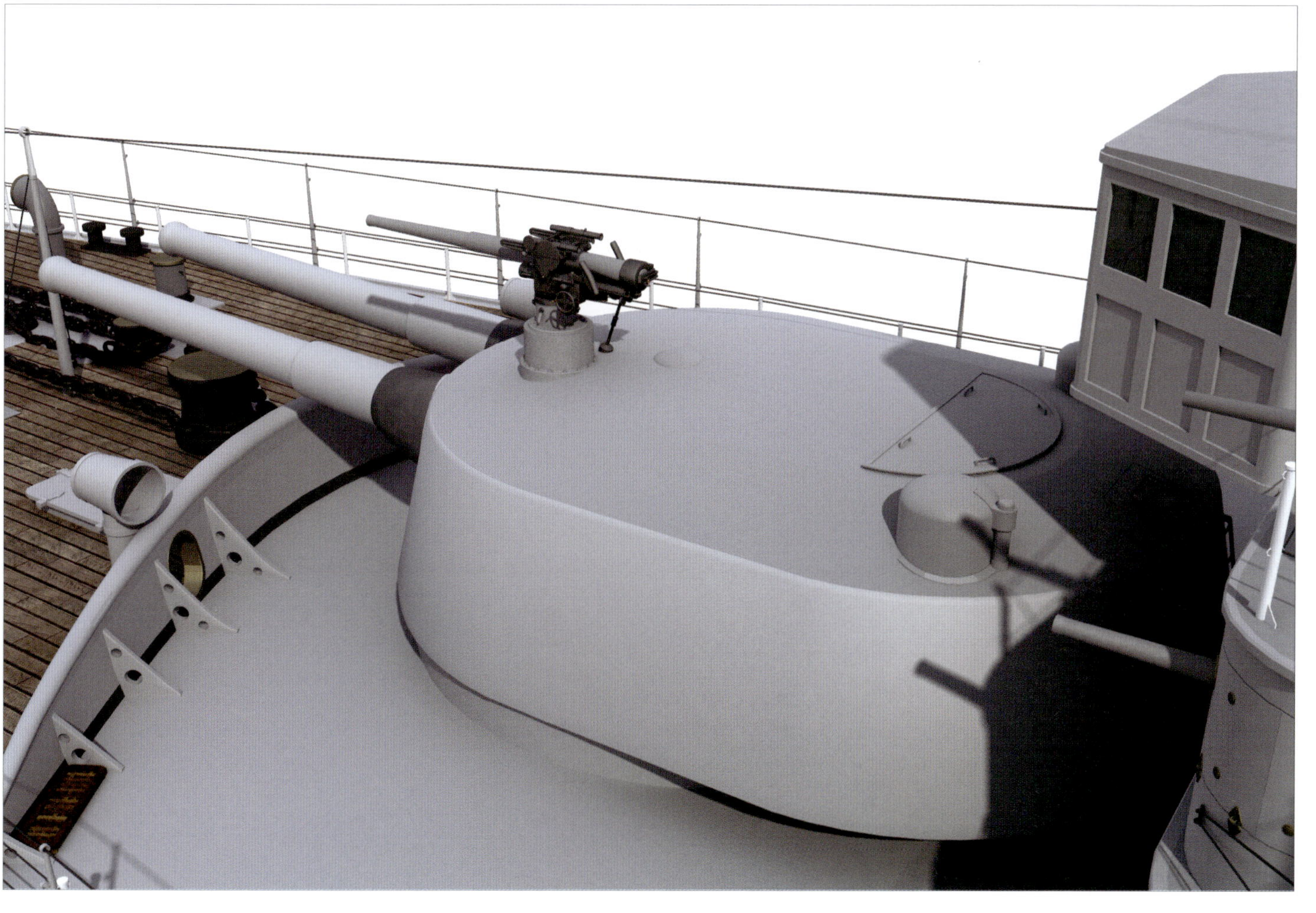

Overall view of the side 190mm armoured turret.

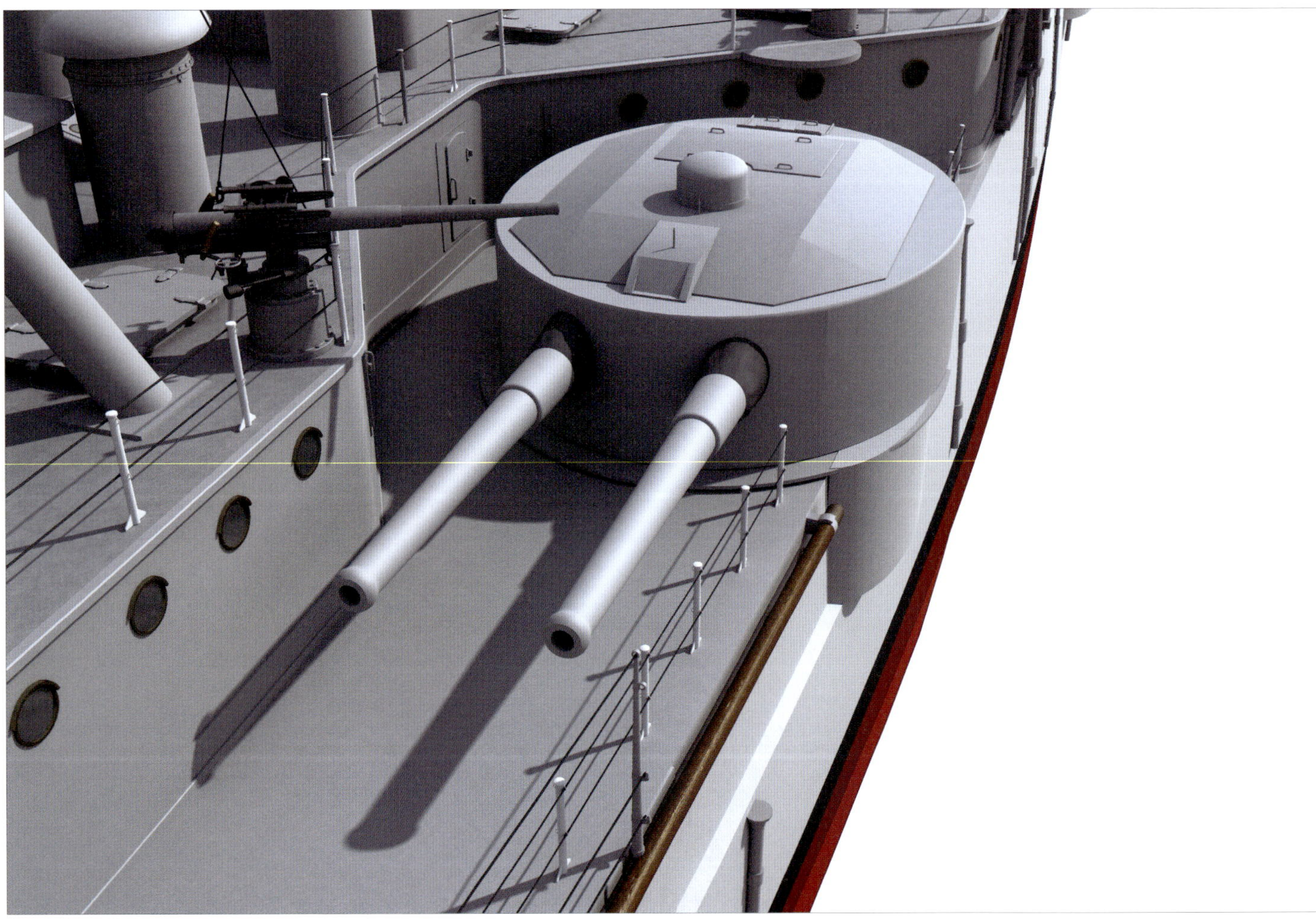

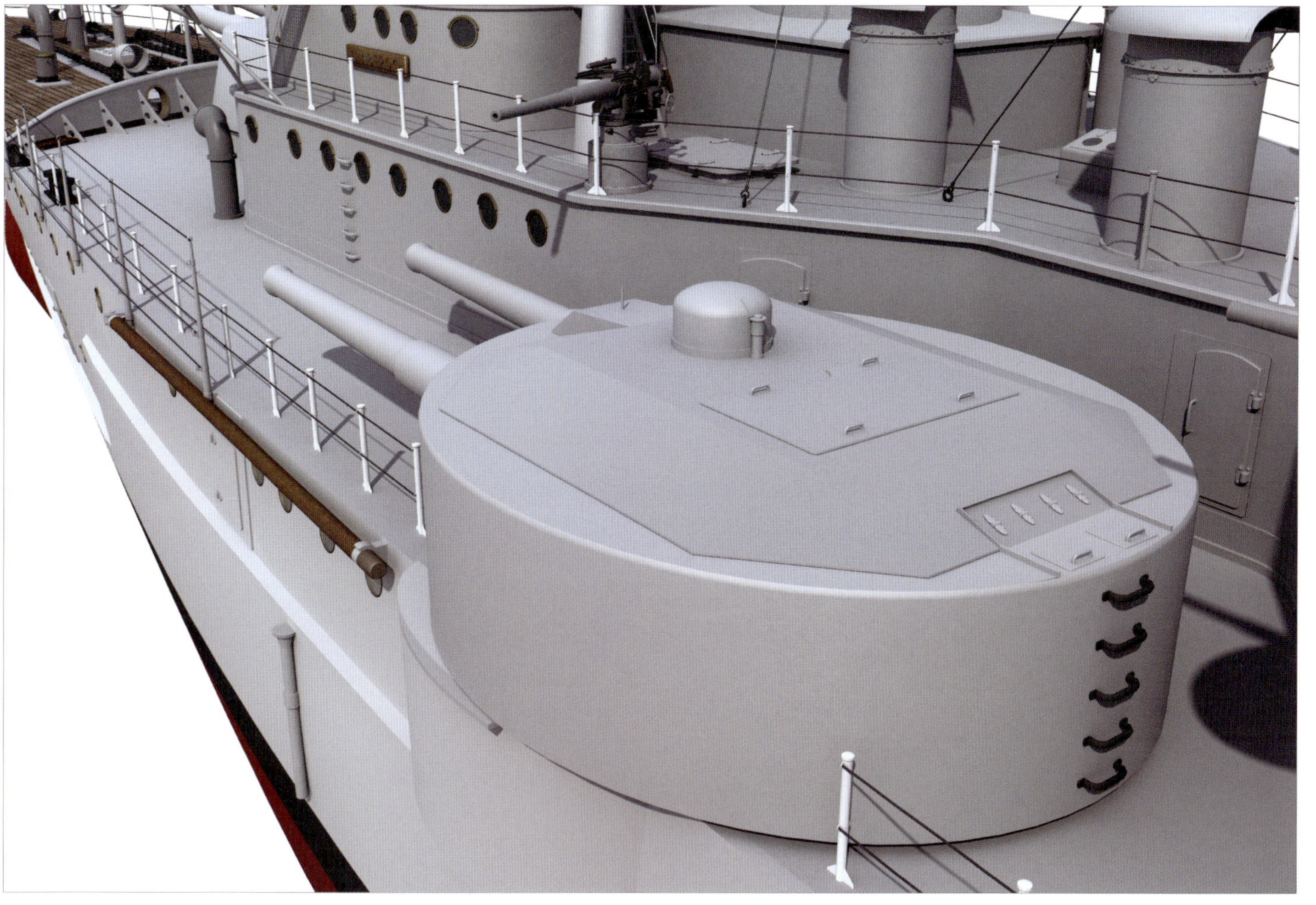

Overall view of the two side 190mm armoured turrets.

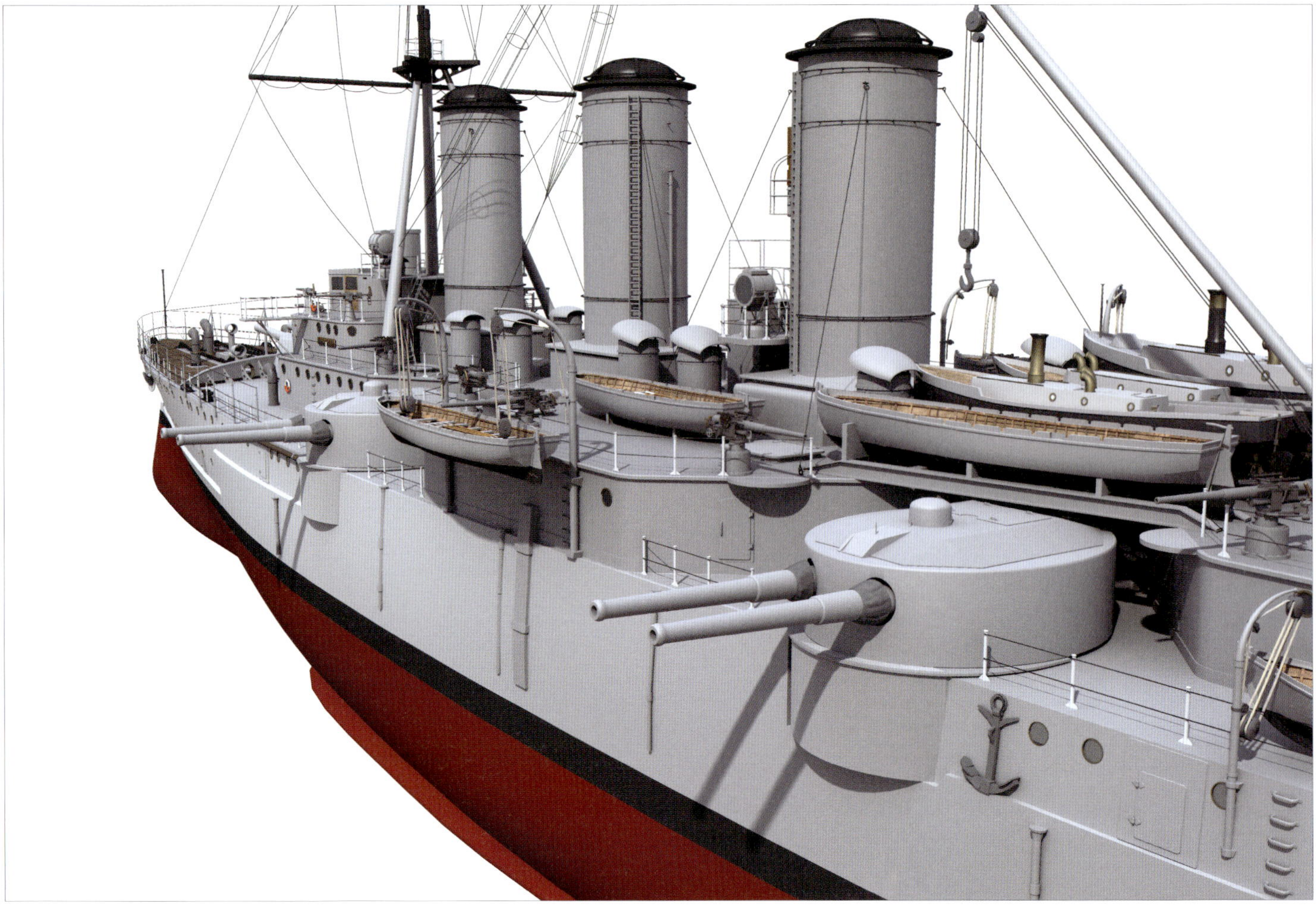

Overall view of the back 234mm armoured turret.

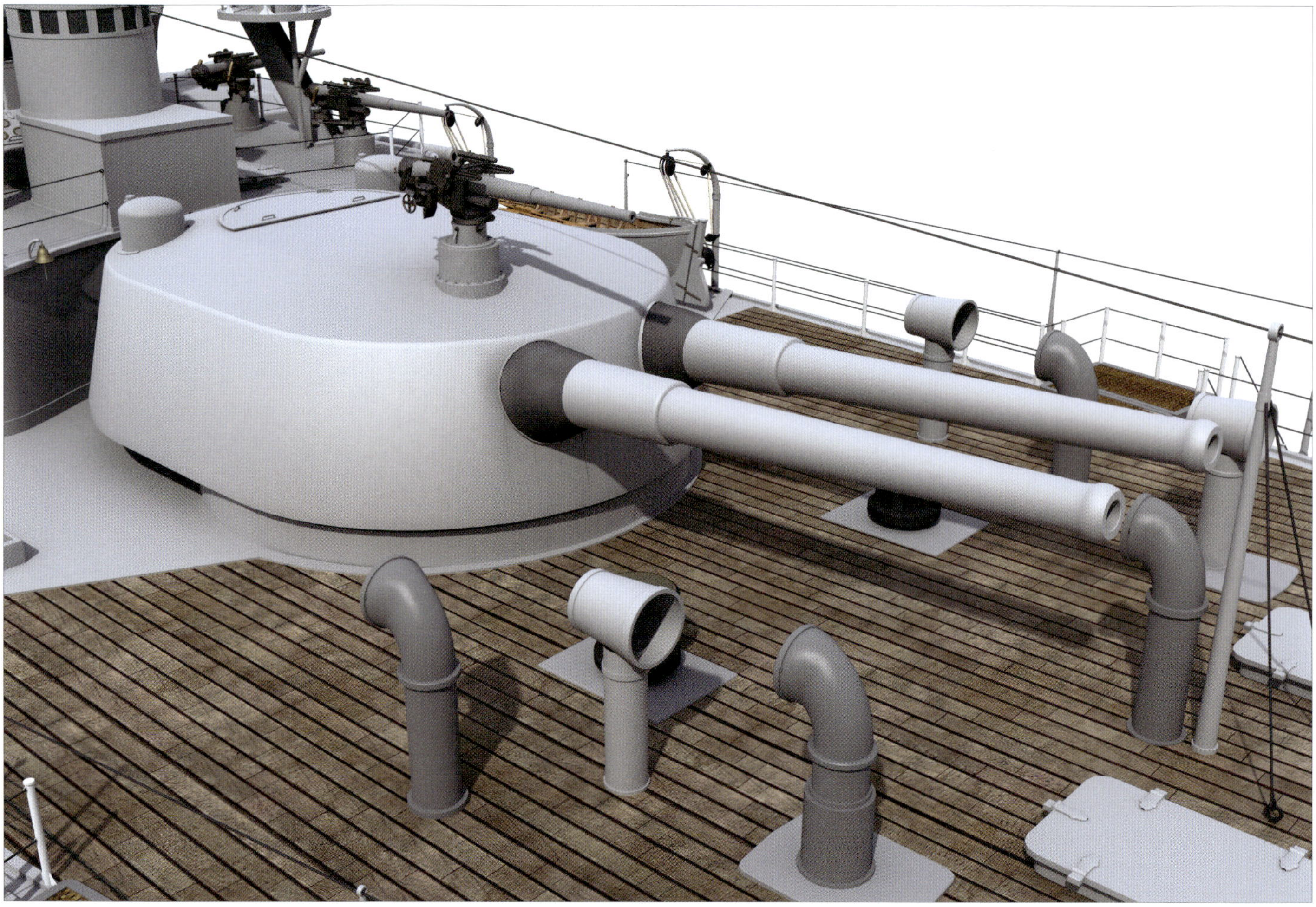

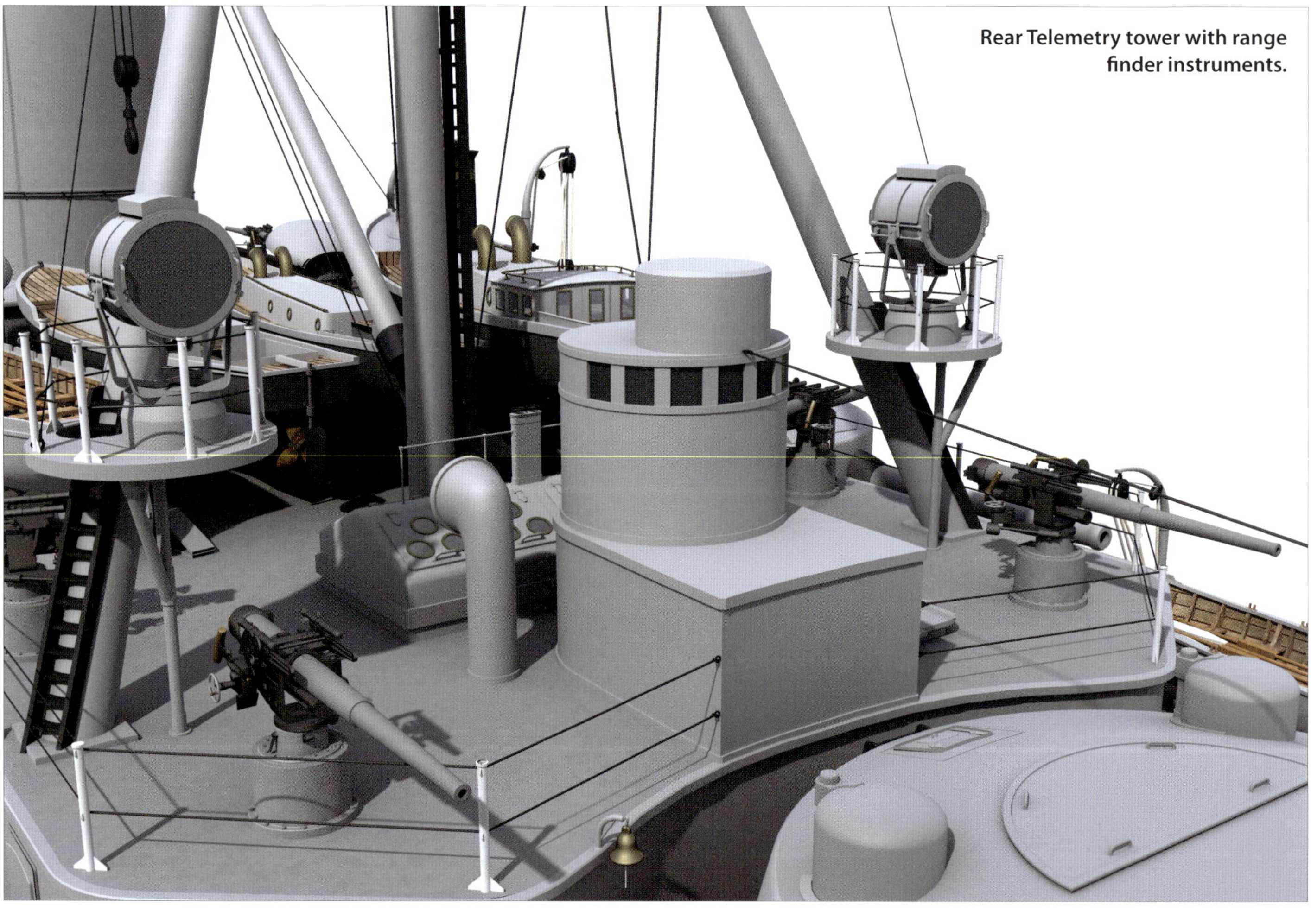

Rear Telemetry tower with range finder instruments.

Overall view of the stern deck.

Overall view of the rear search lights.

Overall view of the Admiral's balcony.

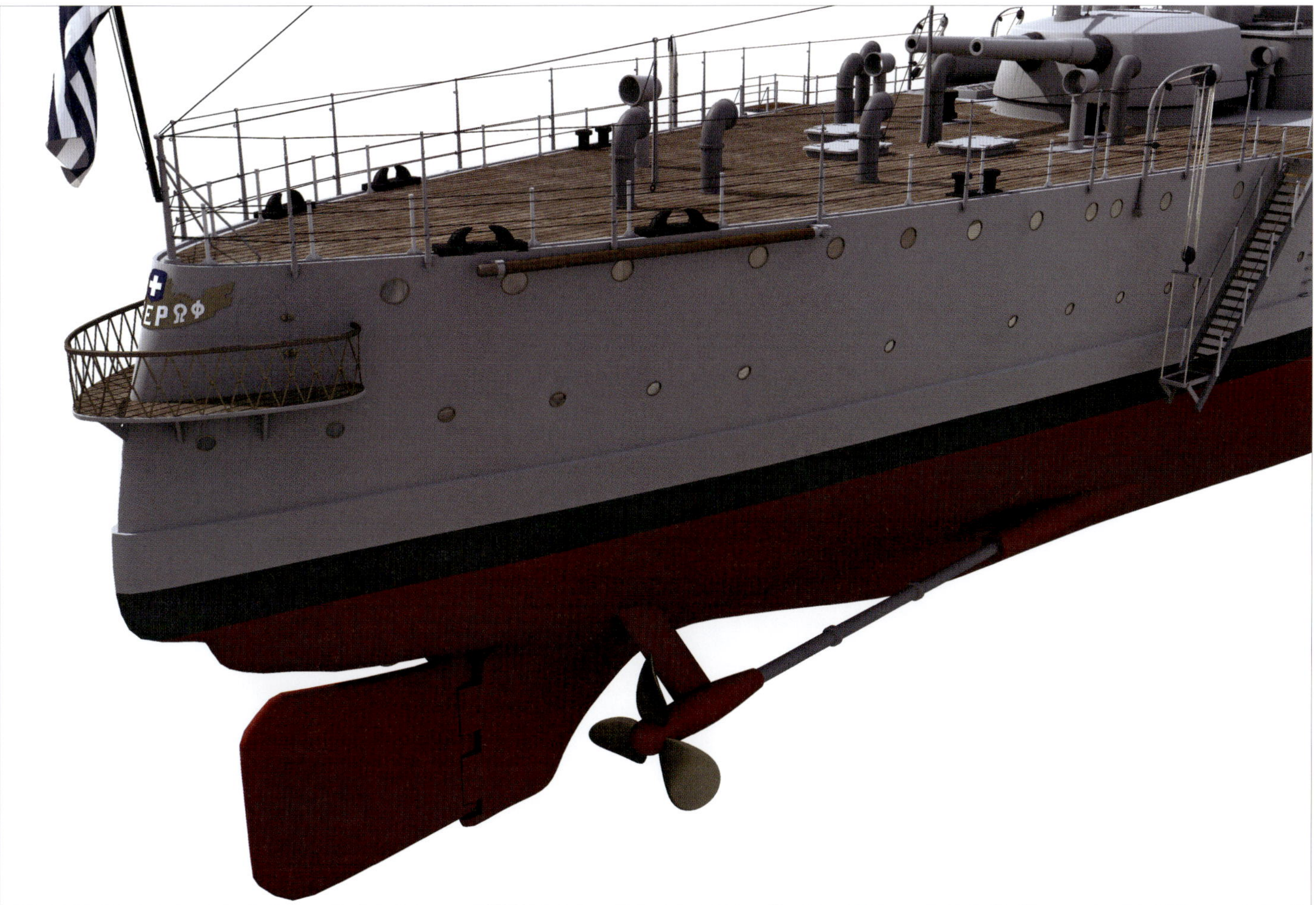

View of Admiral's steam boat (45 ft. pinnace).

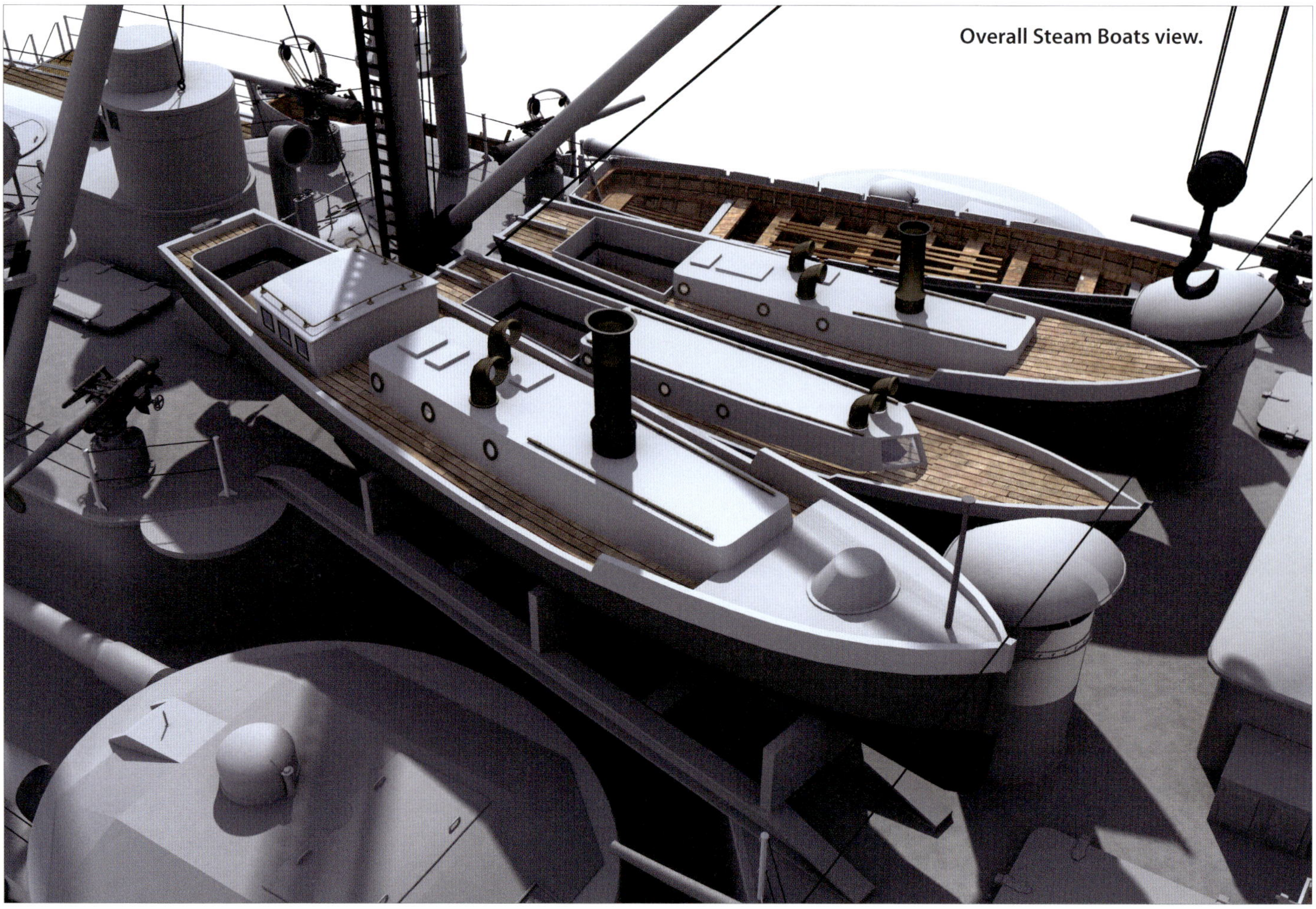

Overall Steam Boats view.

The bell of the ship located in the rear part of the deck.

External view of the chapelof the ship dedicated to St.Nicholas, patron of the Hellenic Navy.

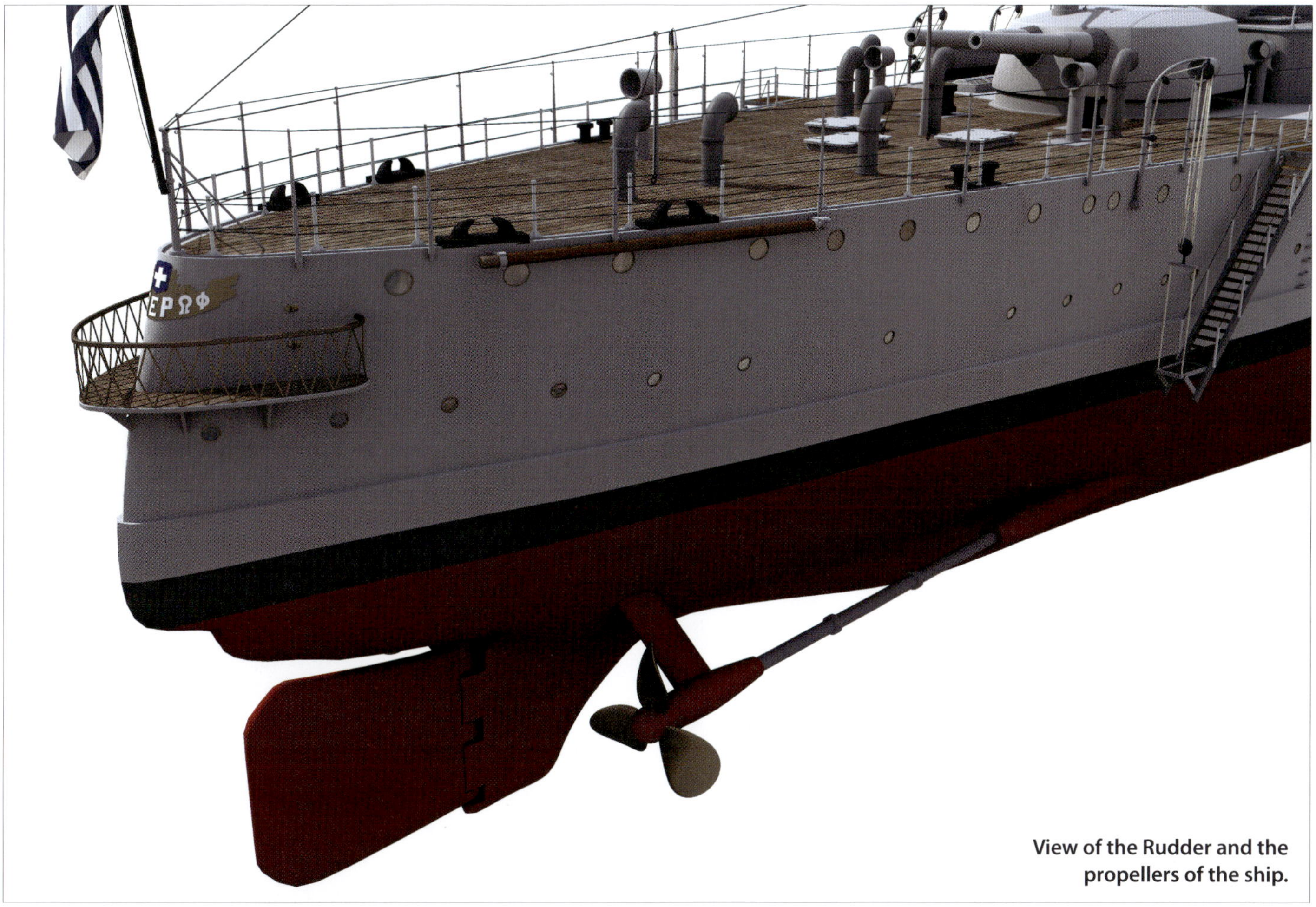

View of the Rudder and the propellers of the ship.

Overall view of ship hull with swinging booms.

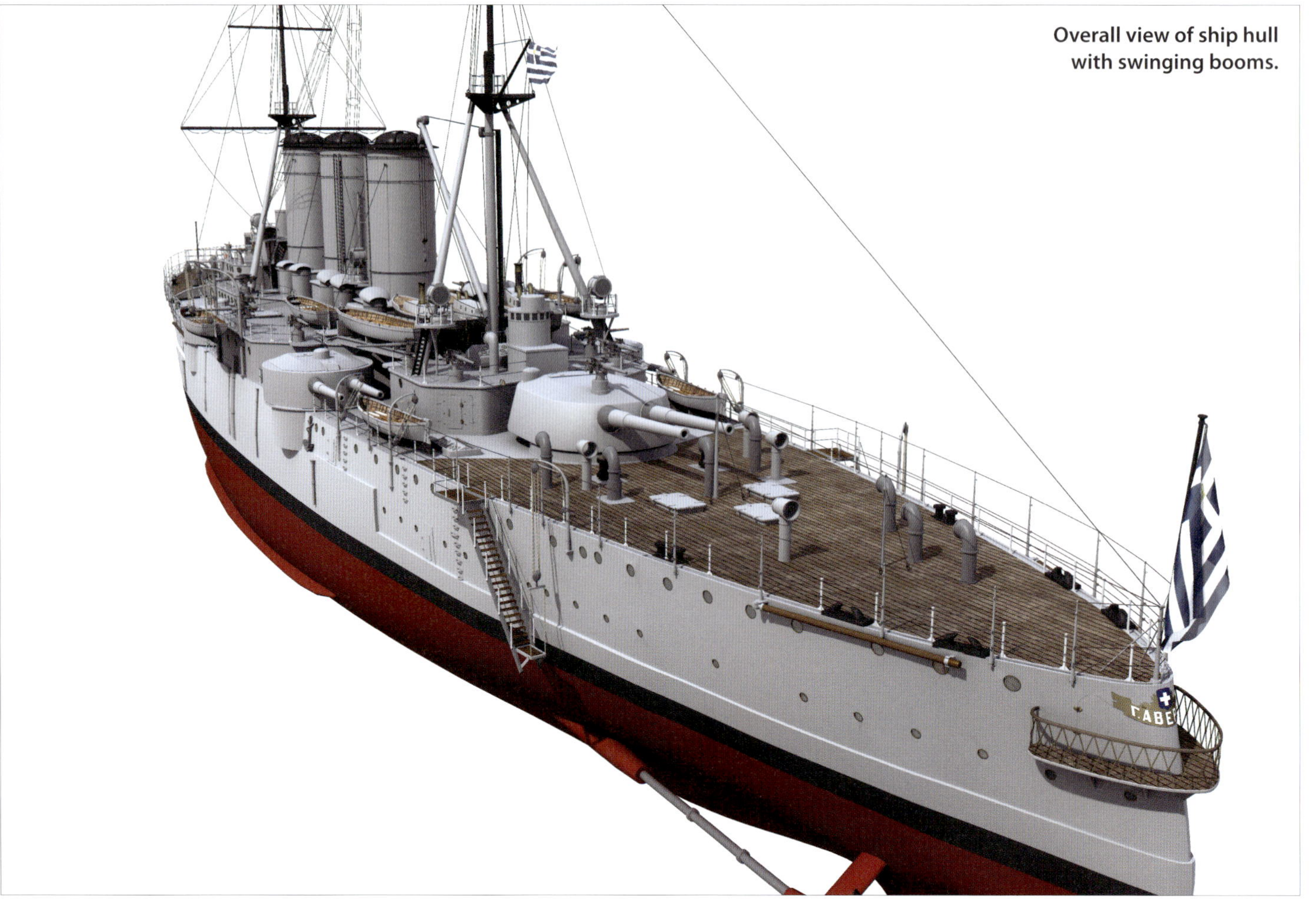

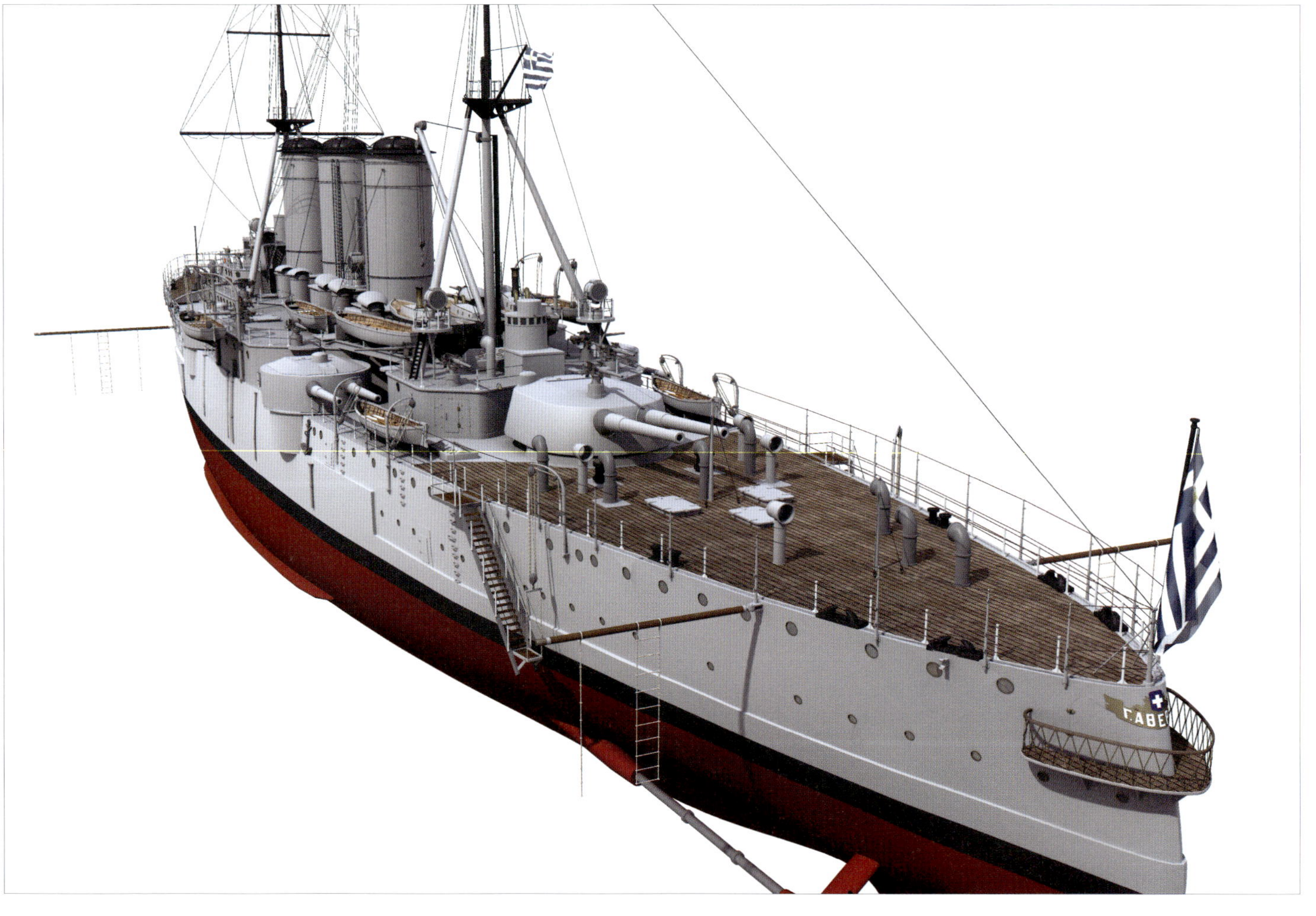

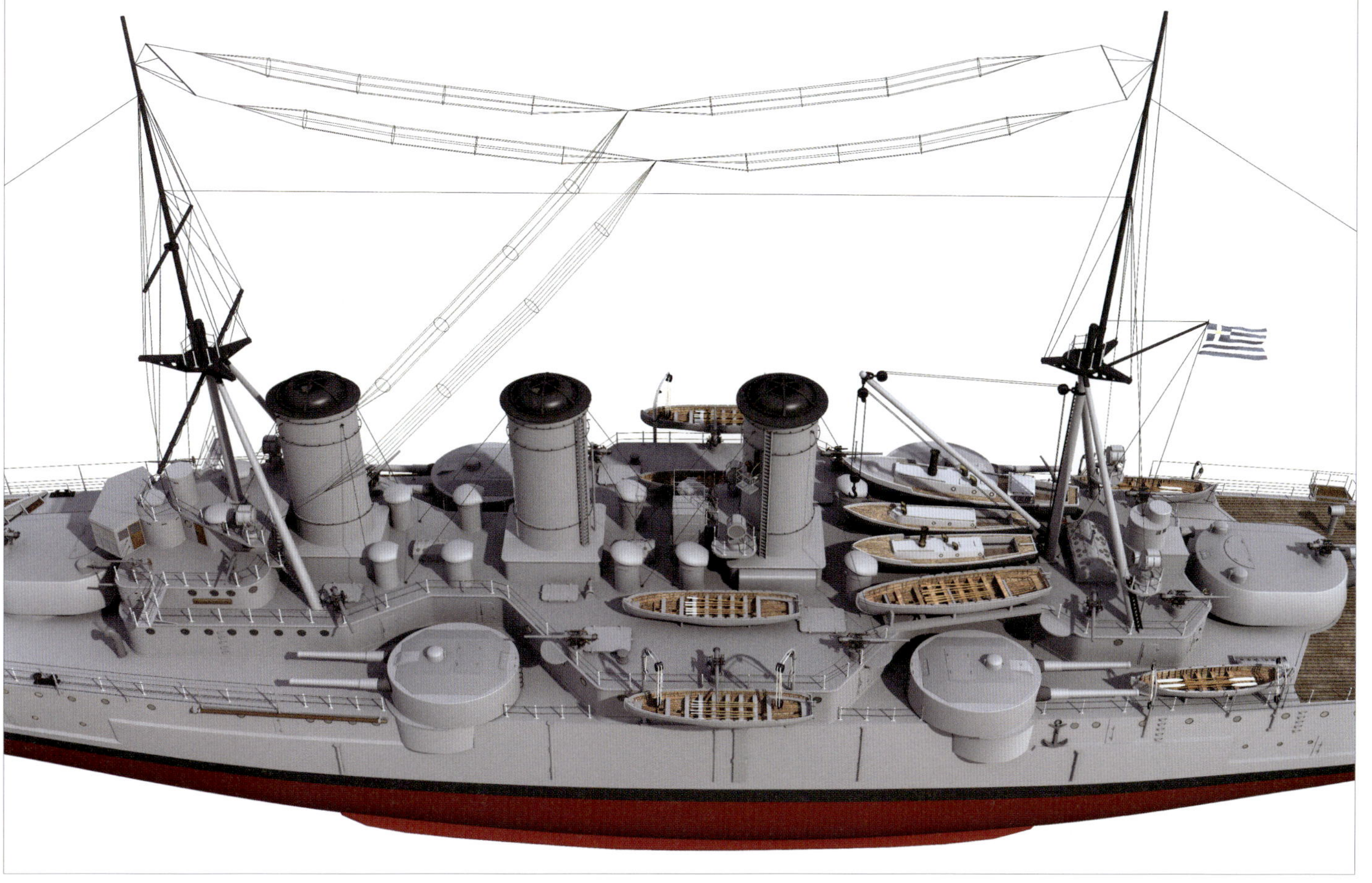

Overall view of the telegraph wires of the ship.

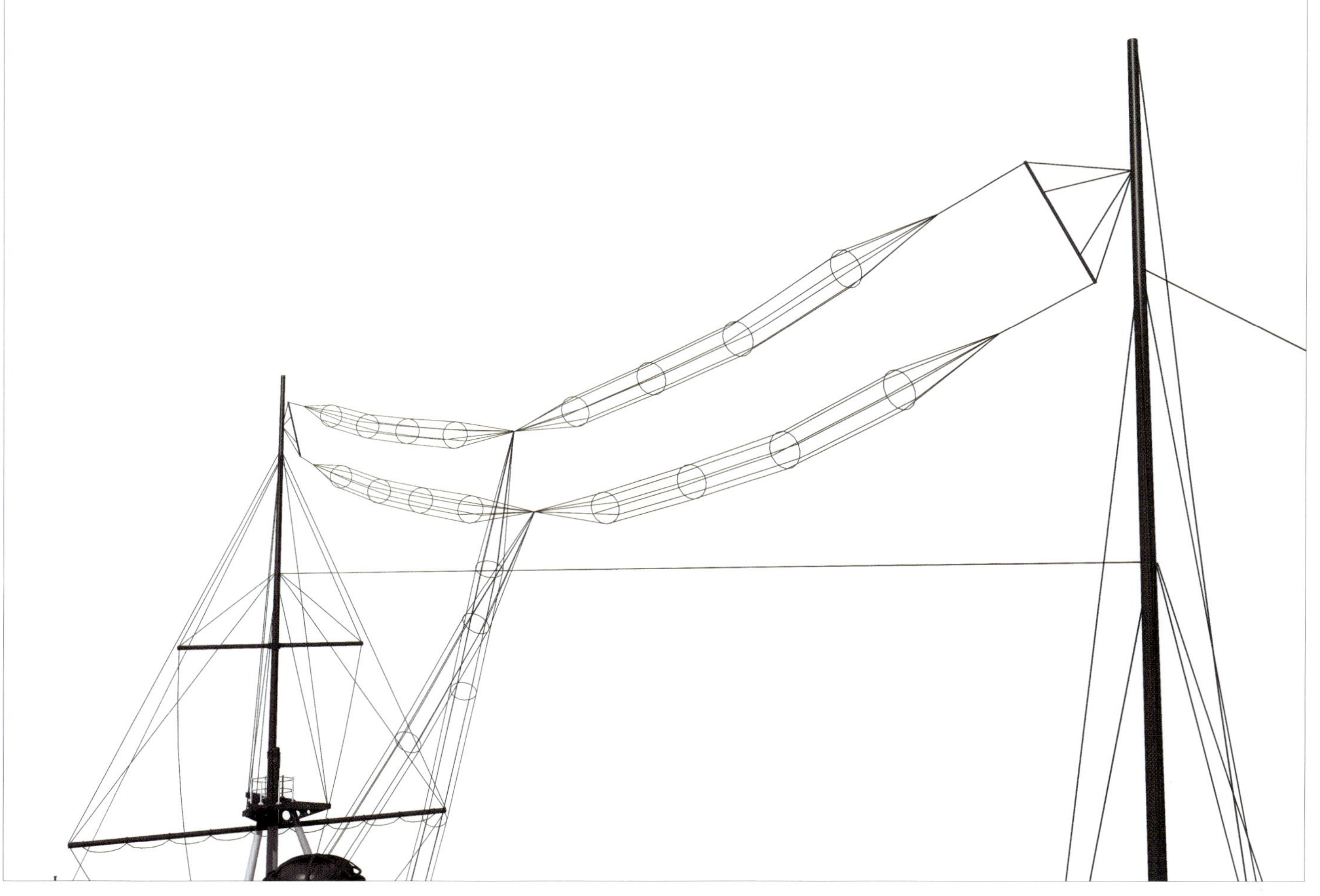

Overall view of the crane boom of the ship.

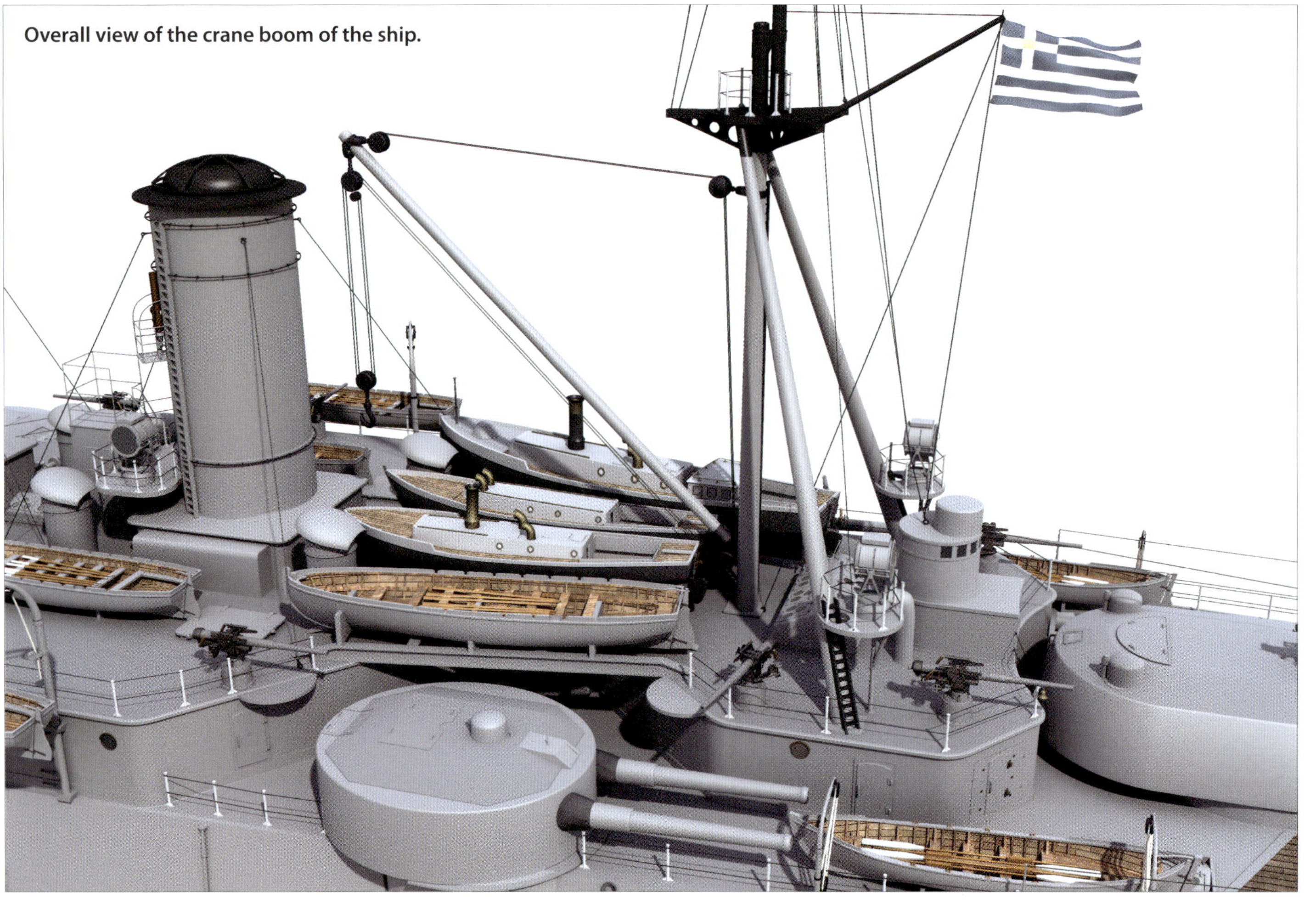

View of the front Mast of the ship.

View of the front Mast Observatory.

Overall view of the front funnel.

View of the middle funnel of the ship.

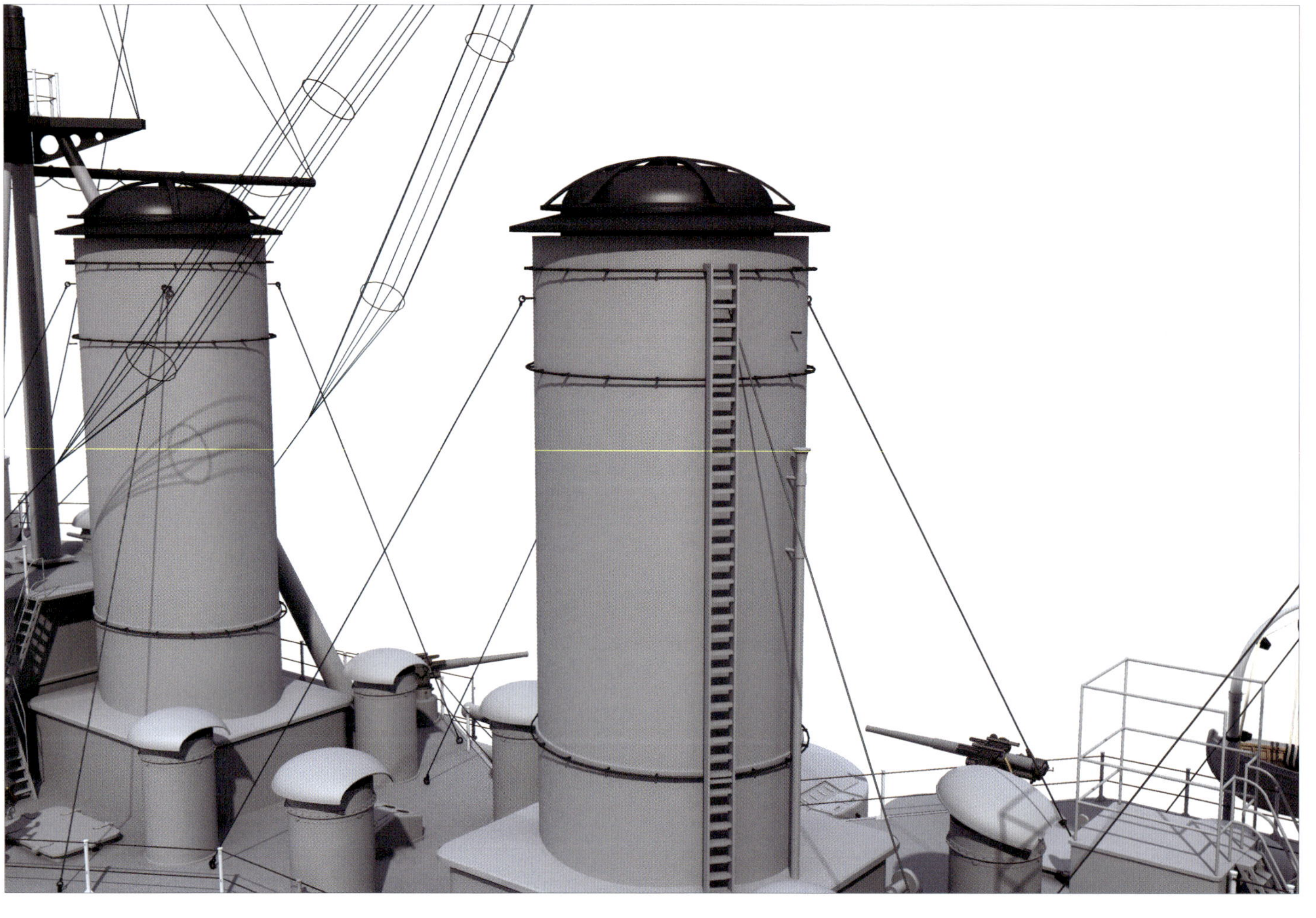

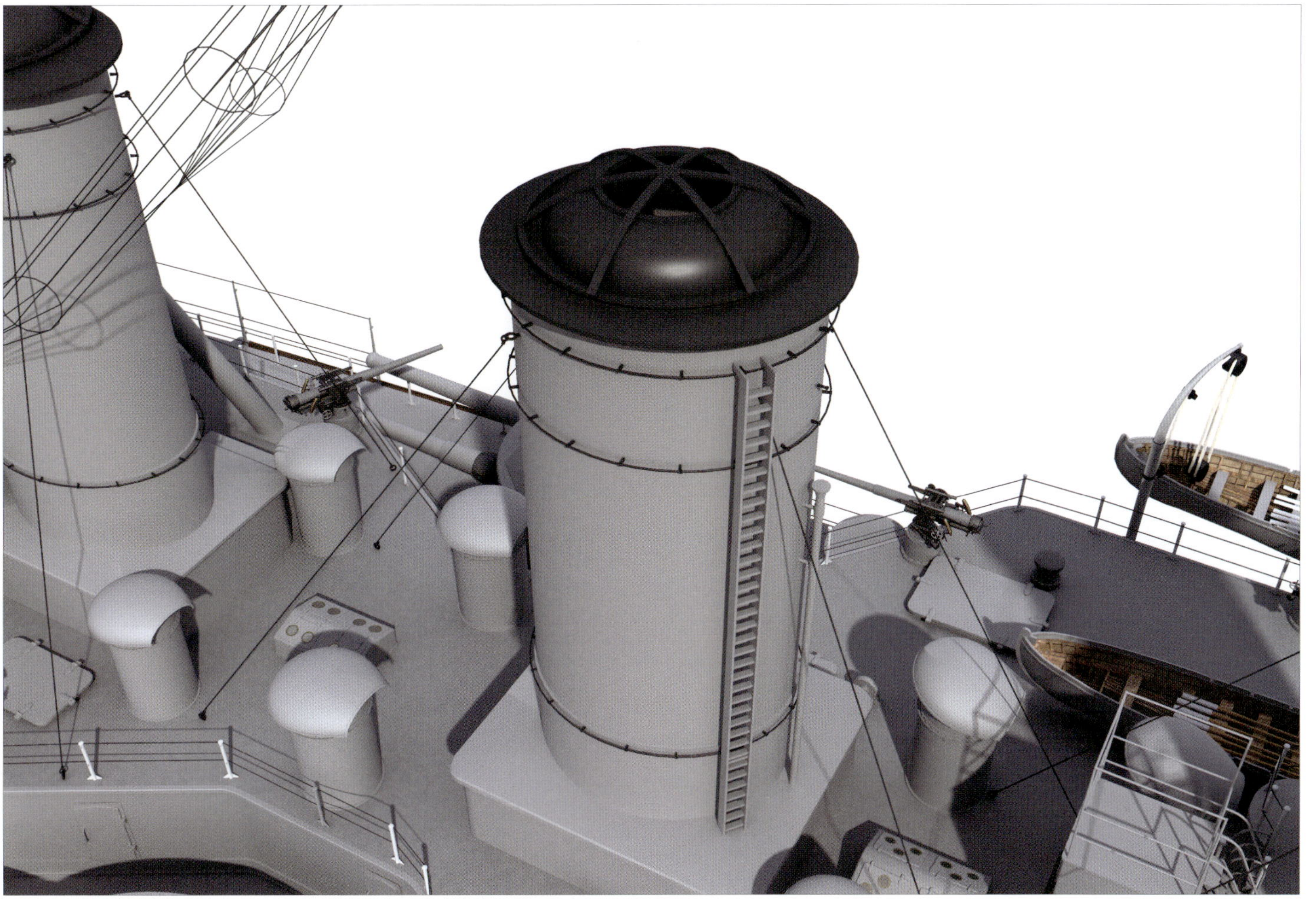

View of the rear funnel of the ship.

Overall view of the funnels and the middle part of the ship.

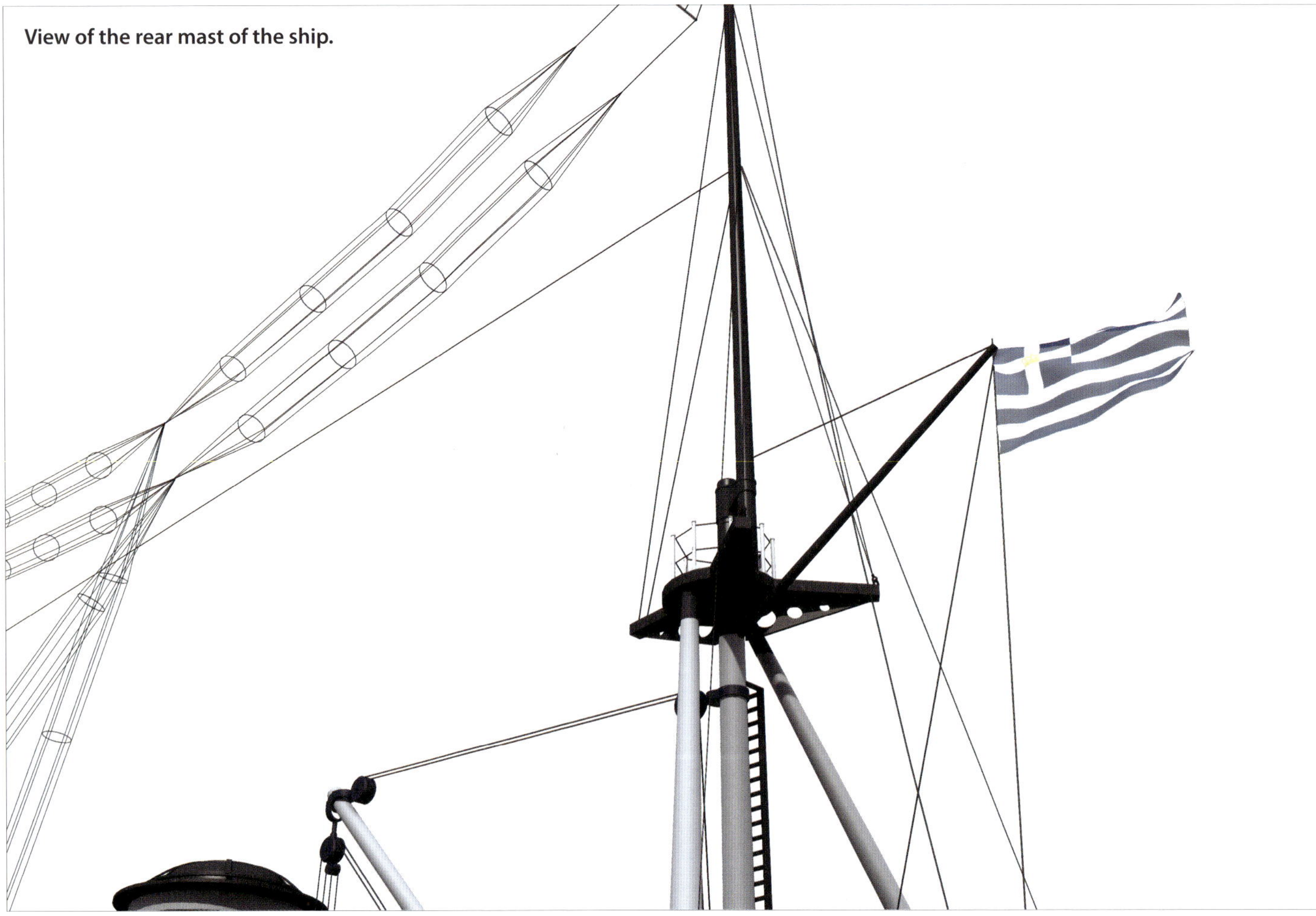

View of the rear mast of the ship.

View of the rear mast observatory of the ship.

View of the front part of the ship.

Overall view of the rear deck of the ship.

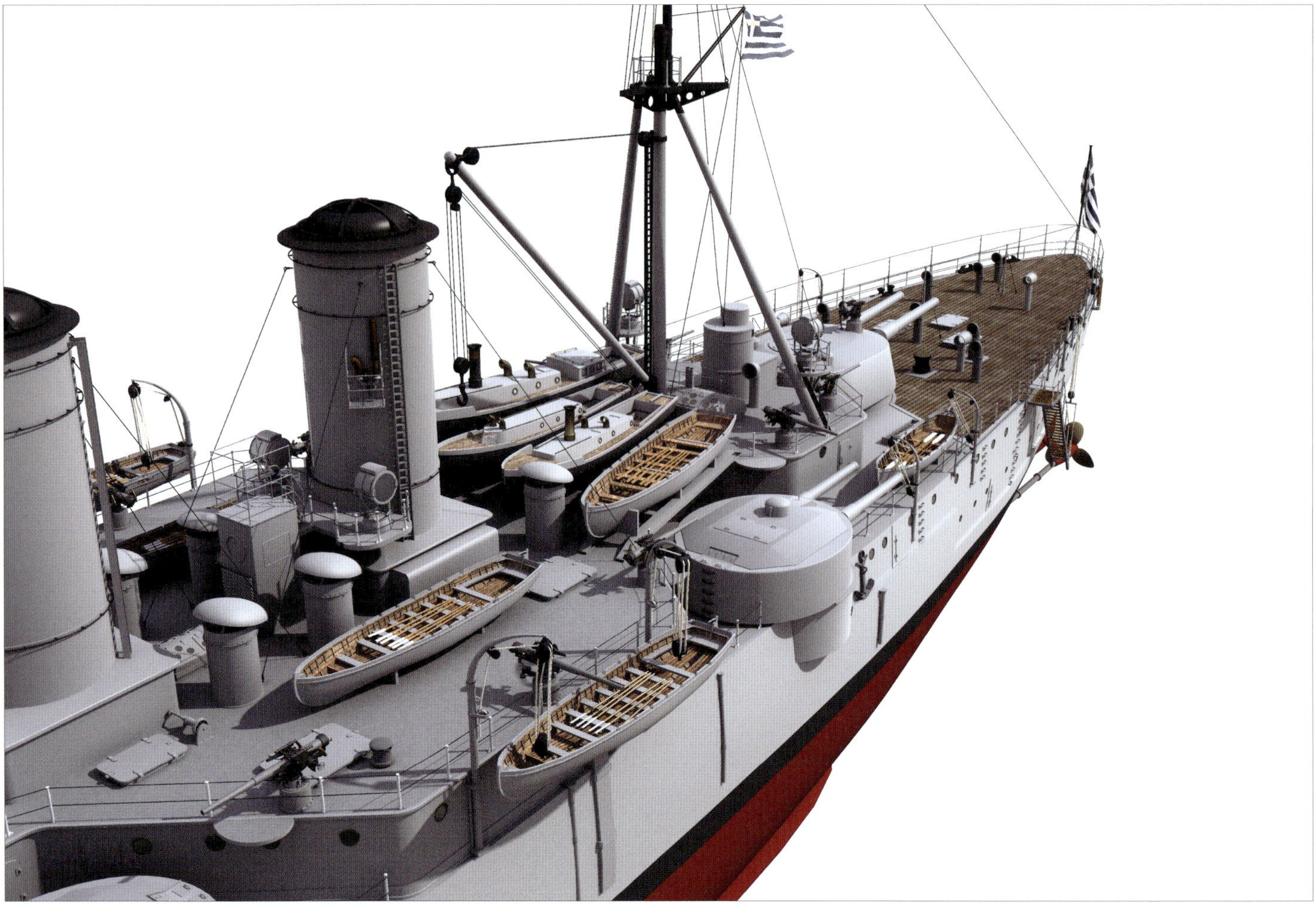

Overall view of the standard and the armored bridge of the ship.

Γ. ΑΒΕΡΩΦ

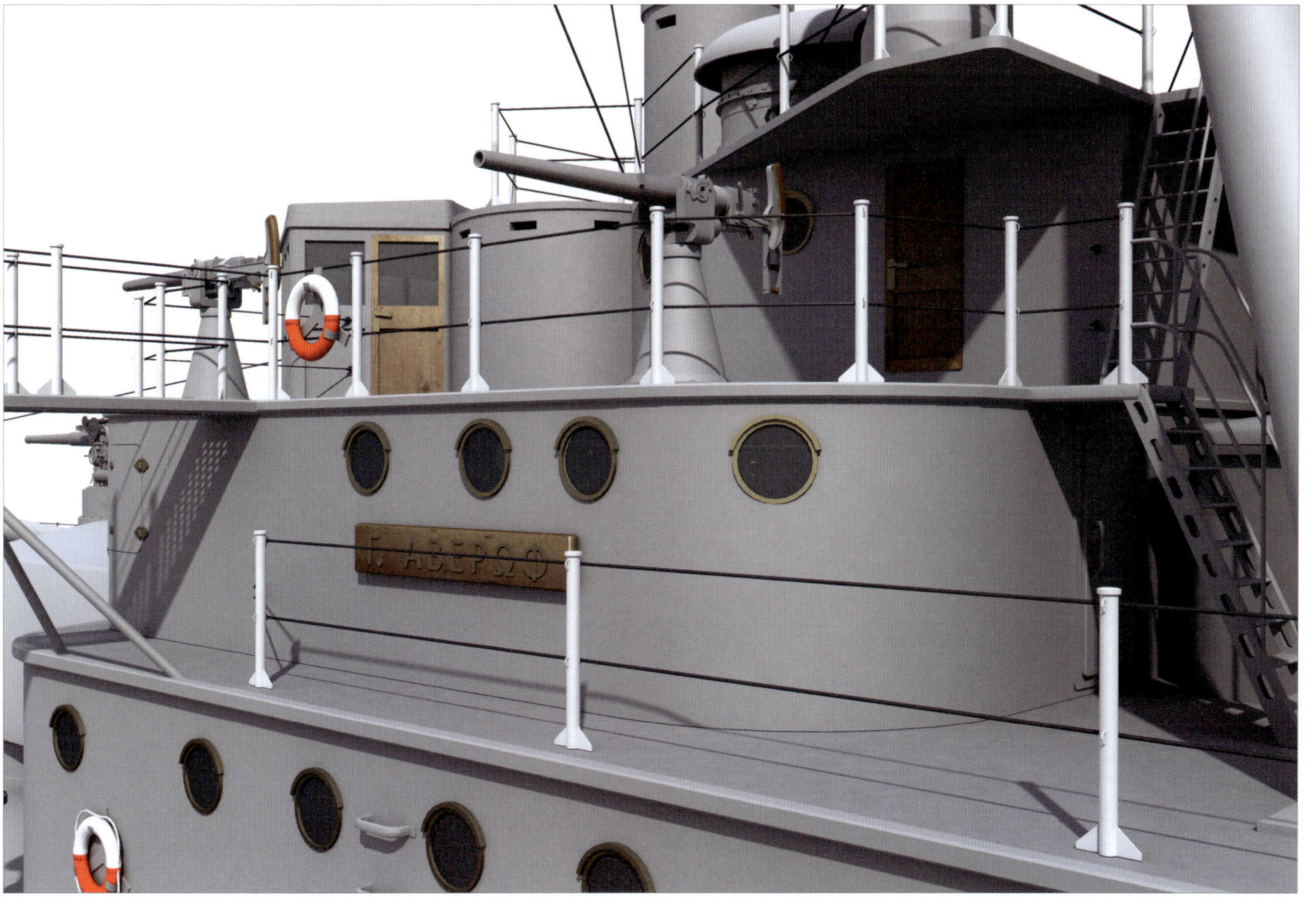
Γ. ΑΒΕΡΩΦ

Front armored telemetry tower with range finder instruments.

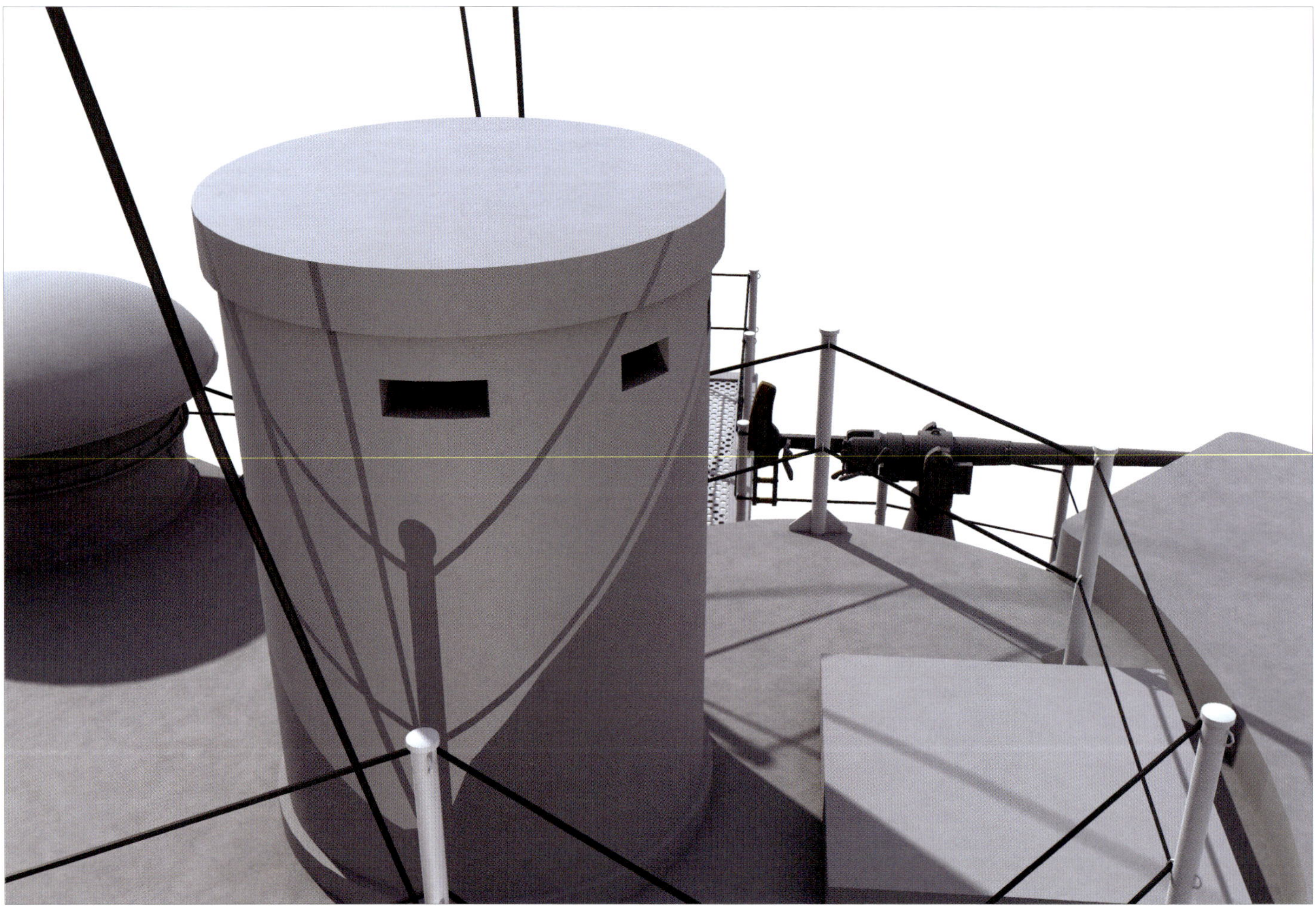

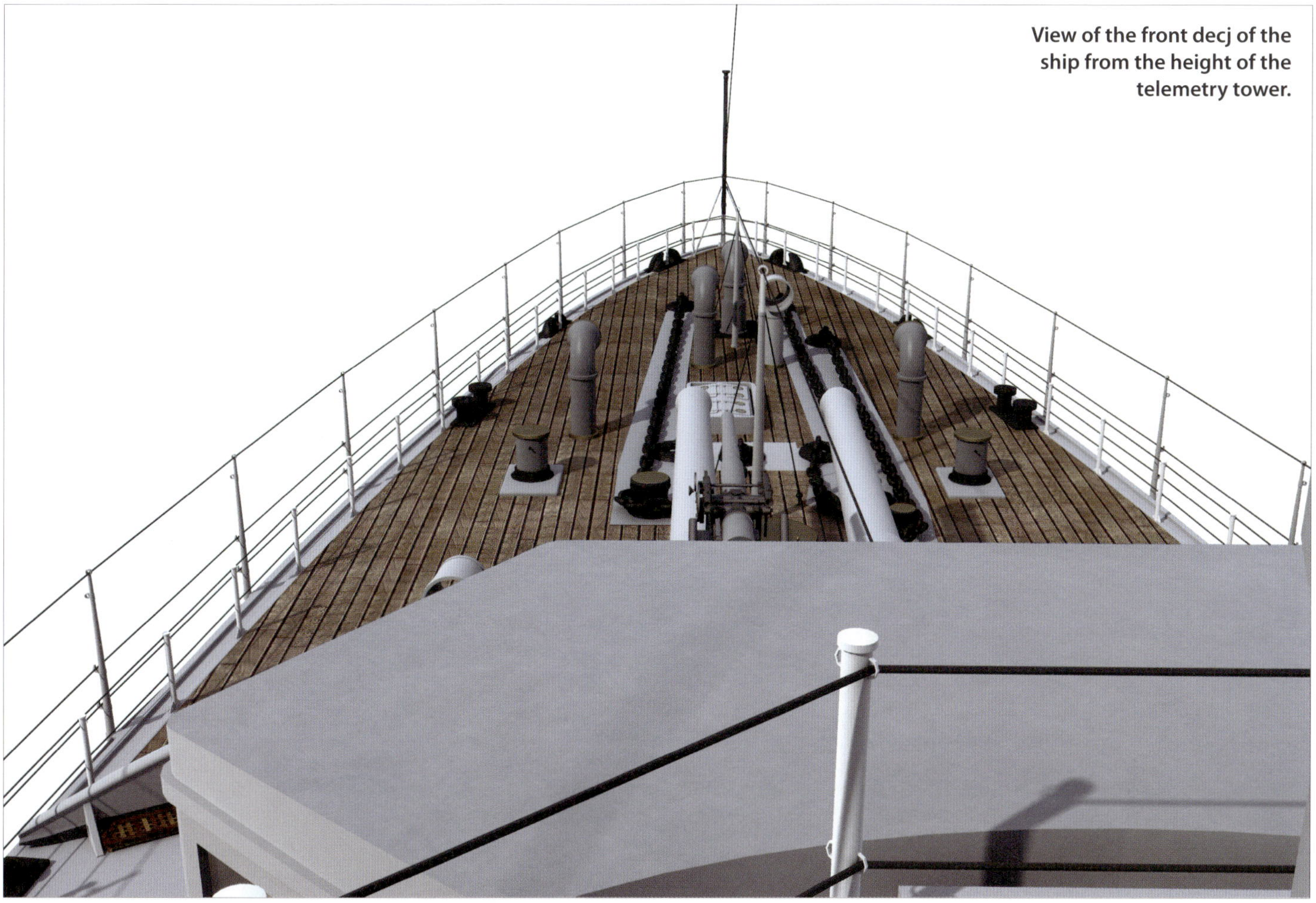

View of the front decj of the ship from the height of the telemetry tower.

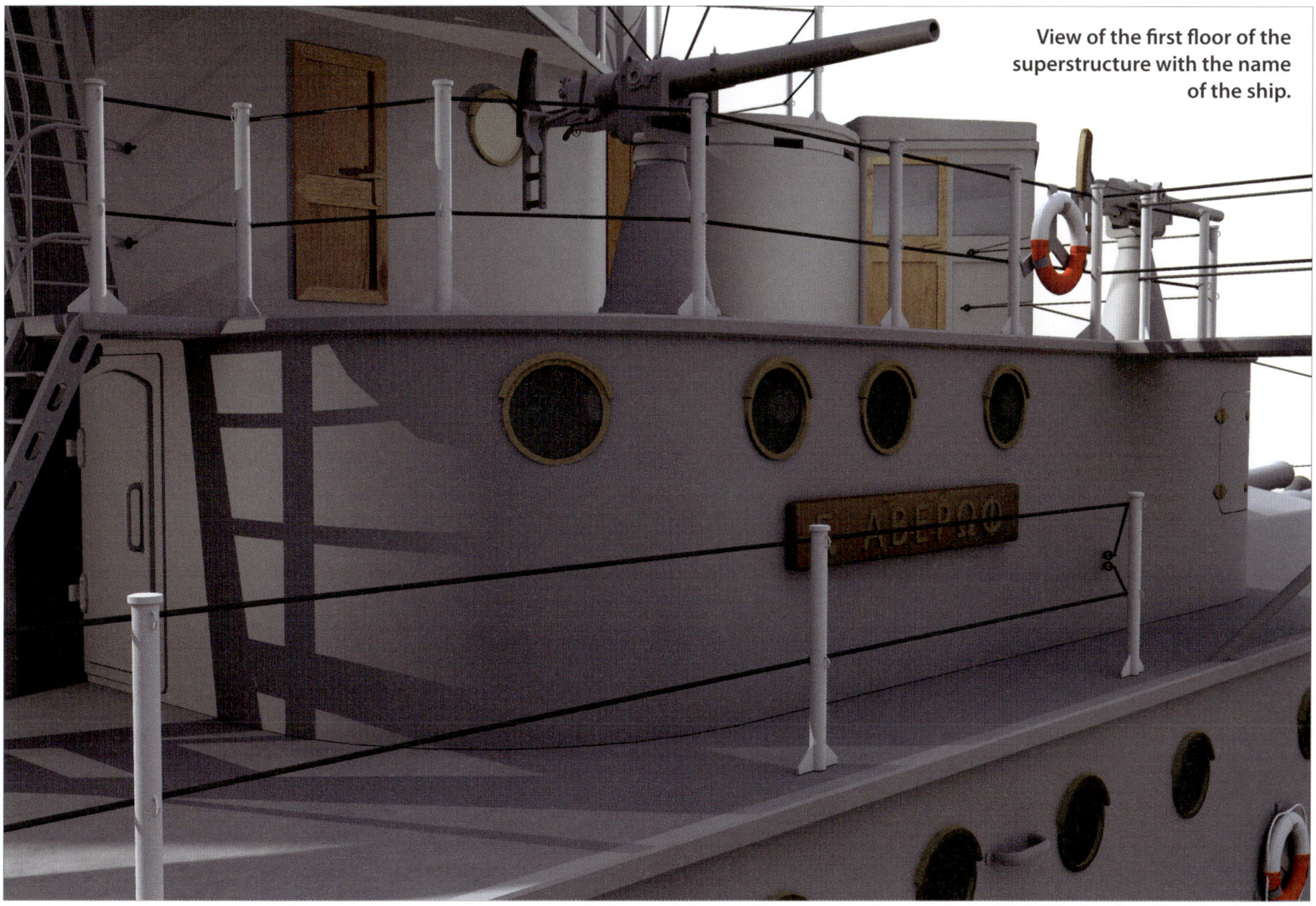

View of the first floor of the superstructure with the name of the ship.

Front view of the first floor of the superstructure with 76mm gun.

Overall view of the front turret range finder gun.

Overall view of 76mm (3pdr) guns at the middle and rear sections of the superstructure.

ΕΡΩΦ

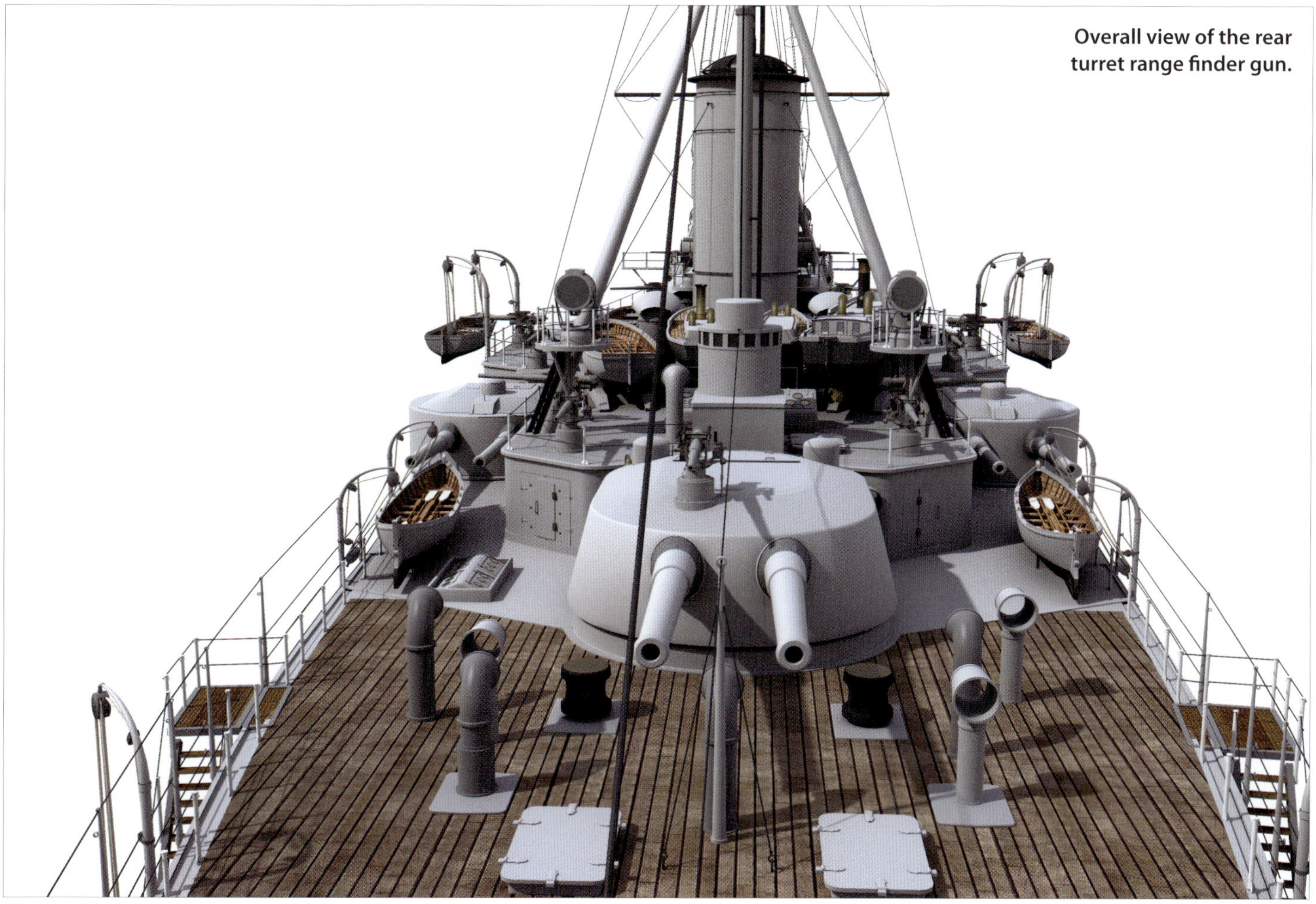

Overall view of the rear turret range finder gun.

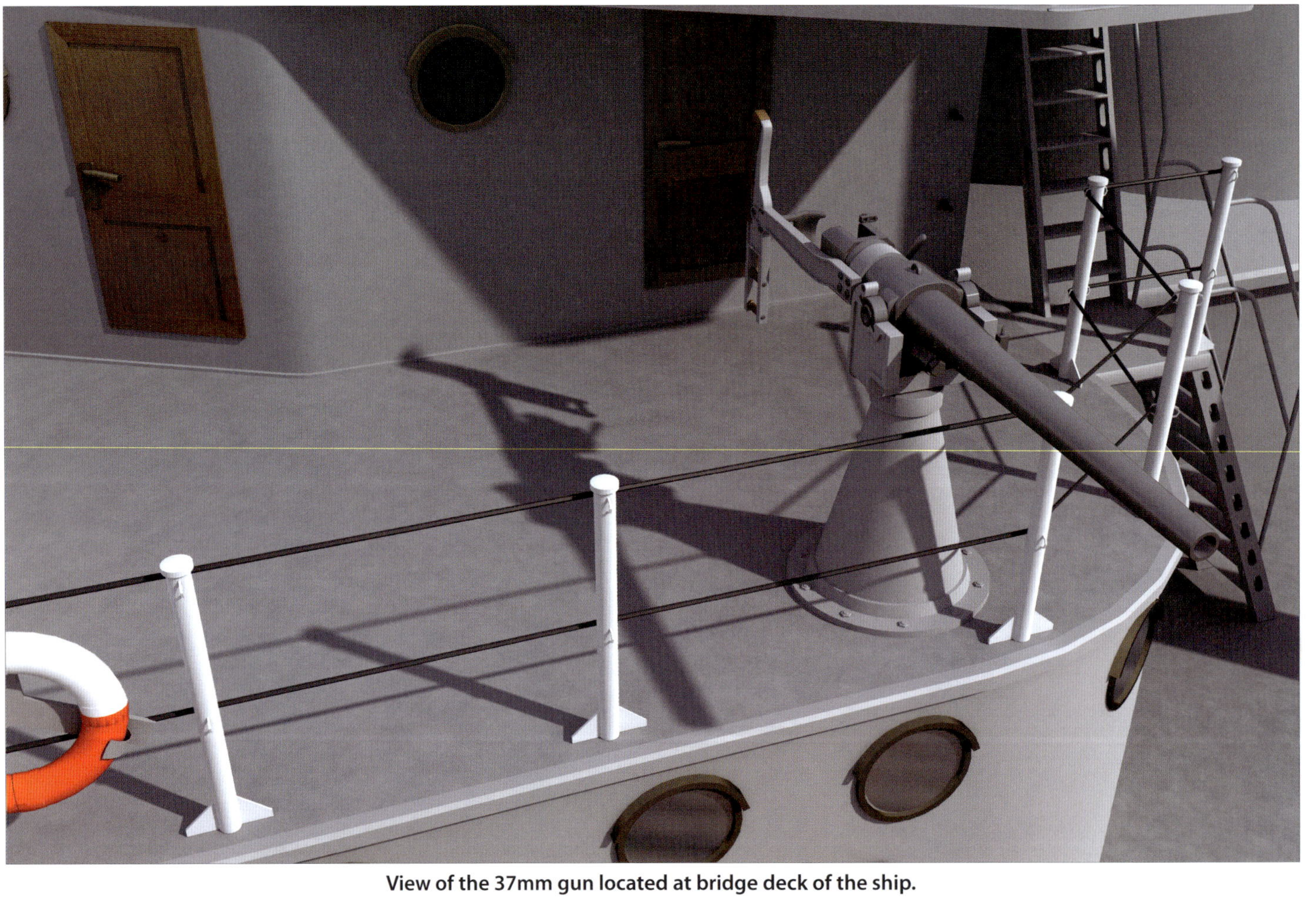

View of the 37mm gun located at bridge deck of the ship.

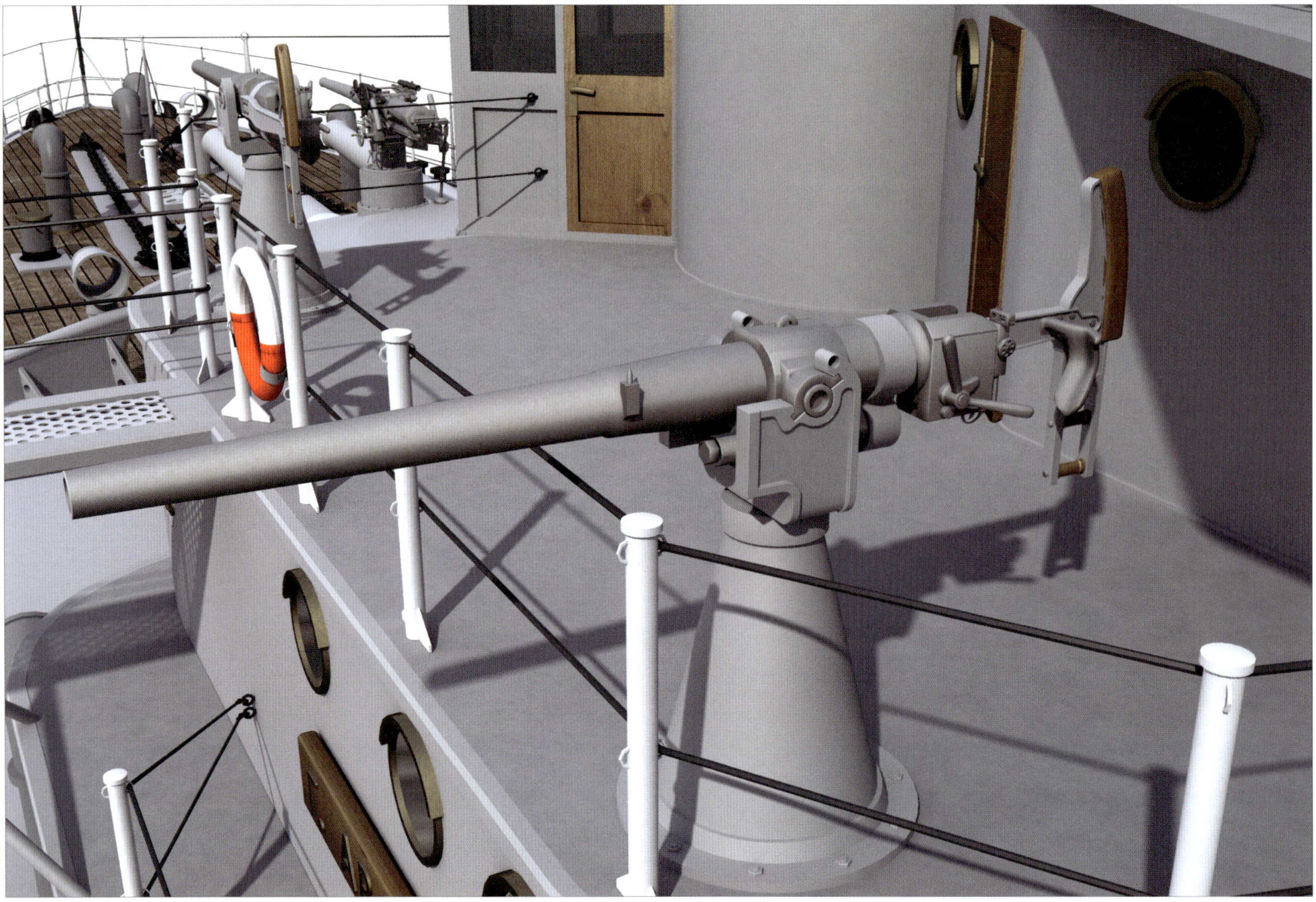

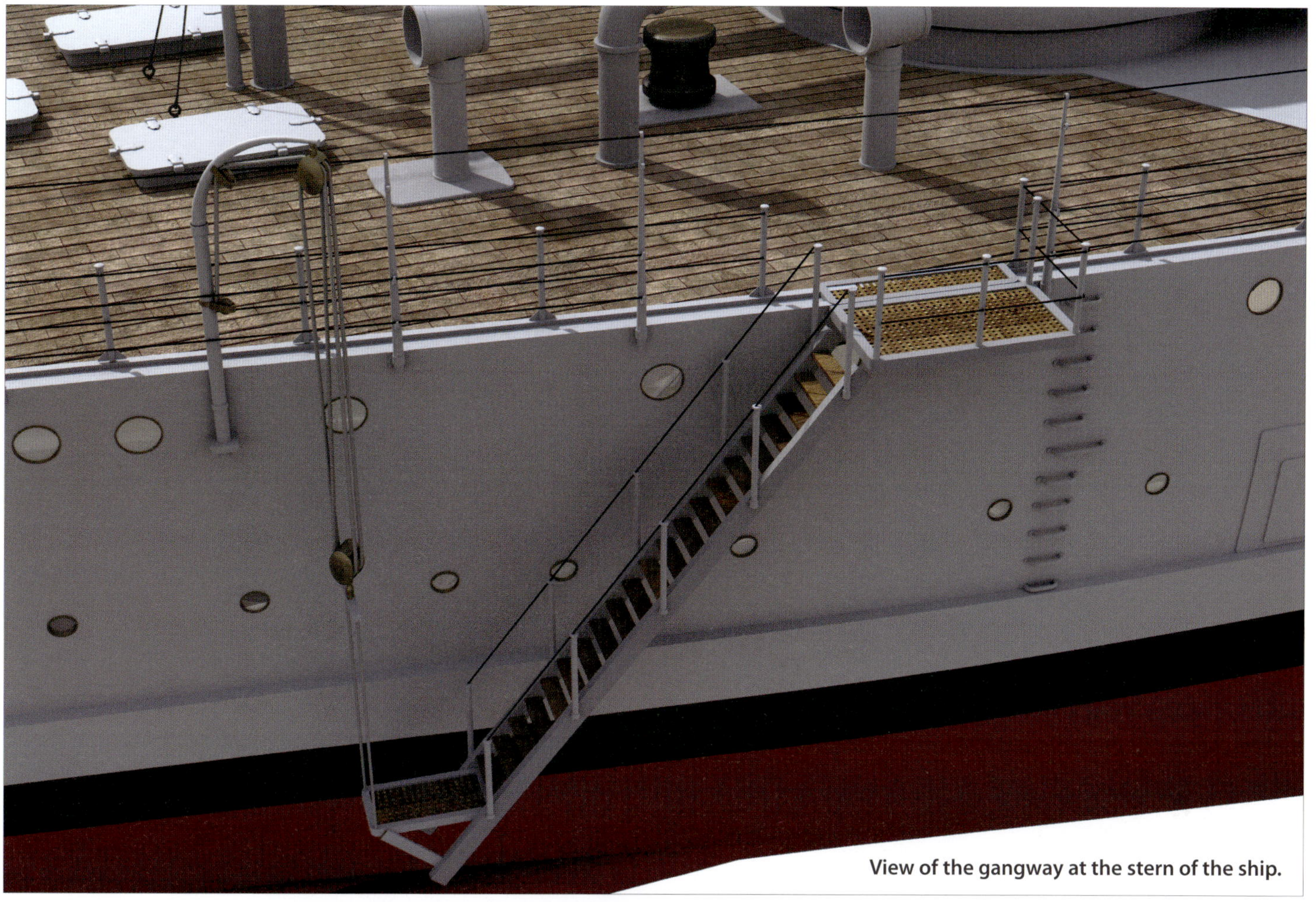

View of the gangway at the stern of the ship.

View of the rotated turrets, as the ship takes position for a "Crossing the T" formation.

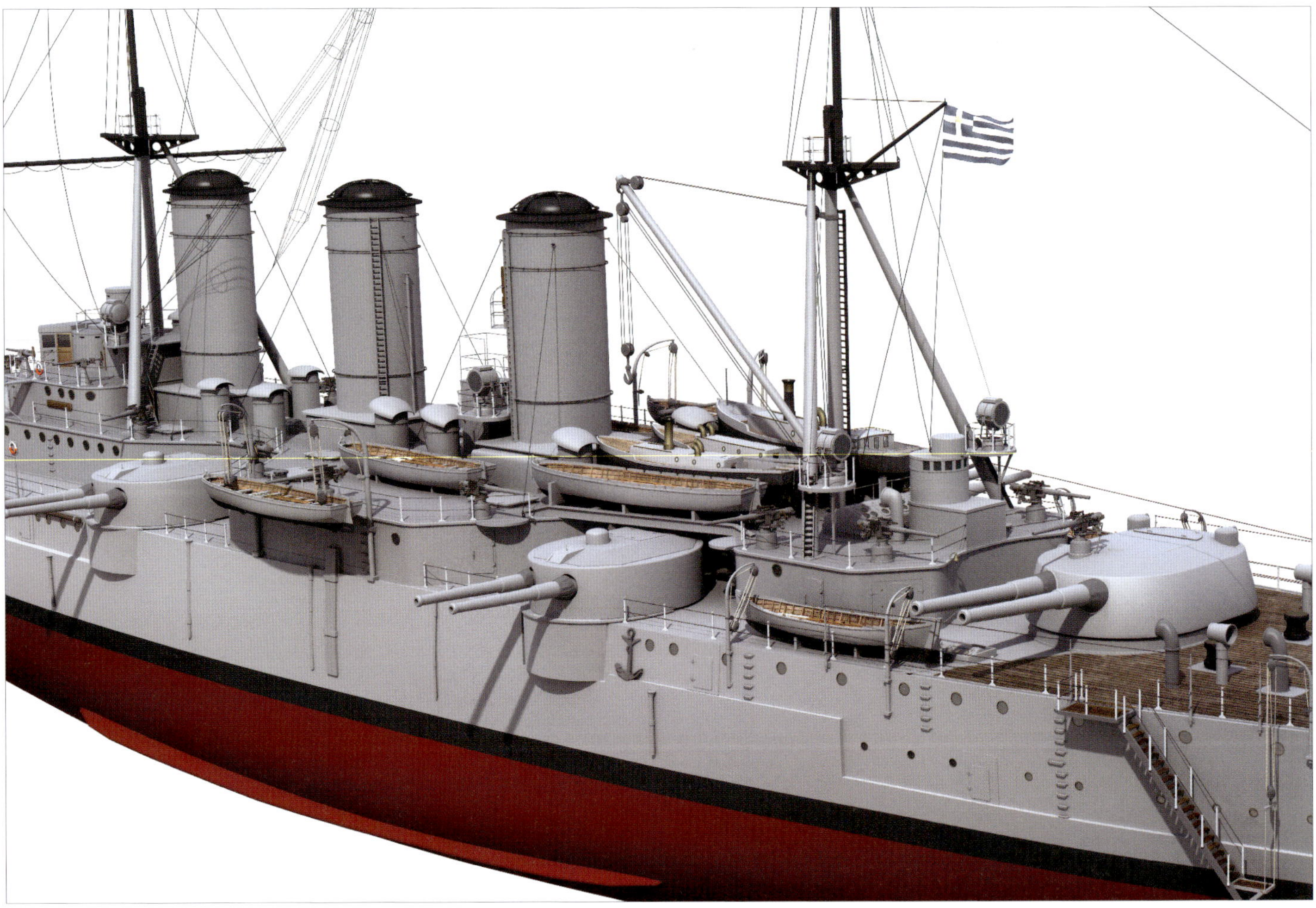

Overall view of the ship as it takes position for a "Crossing the T" formation.

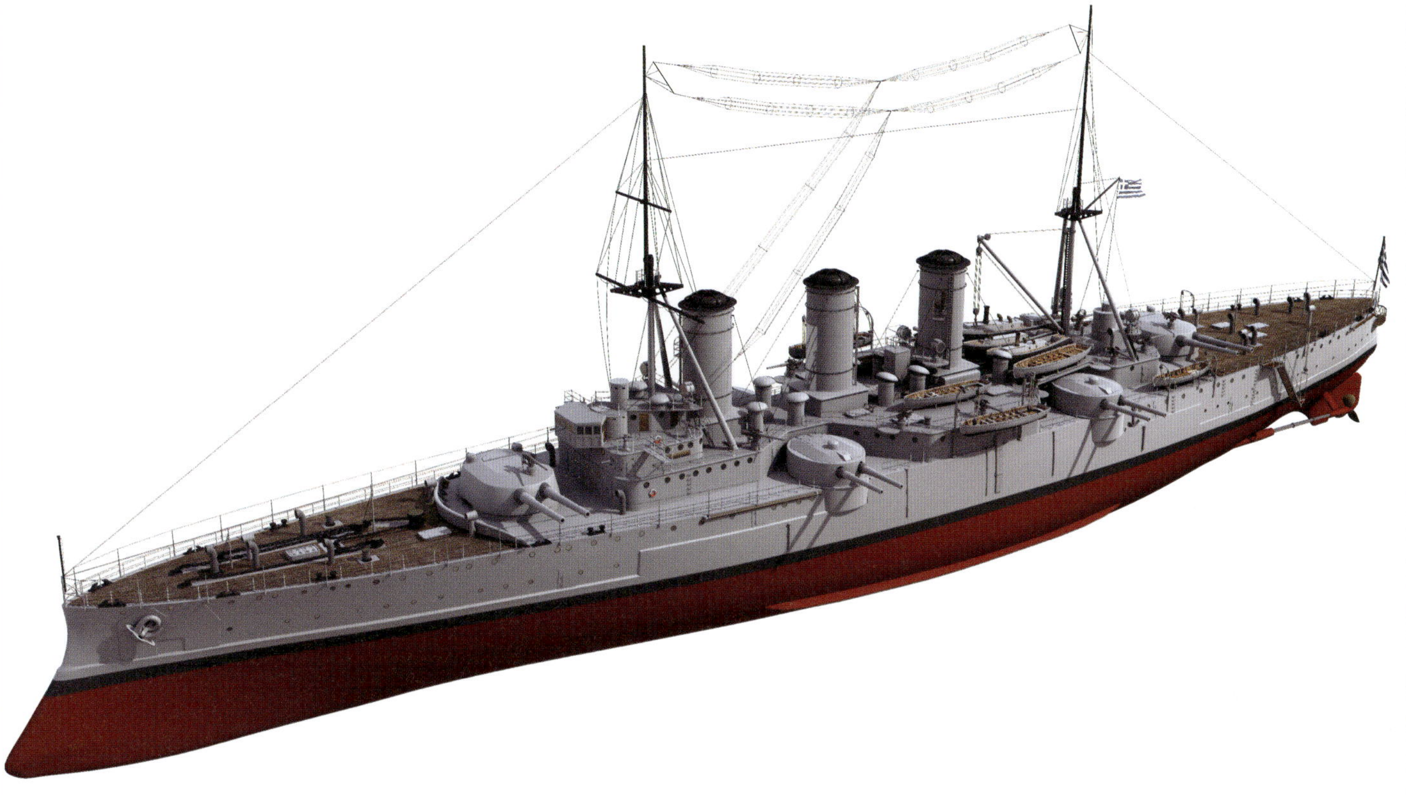

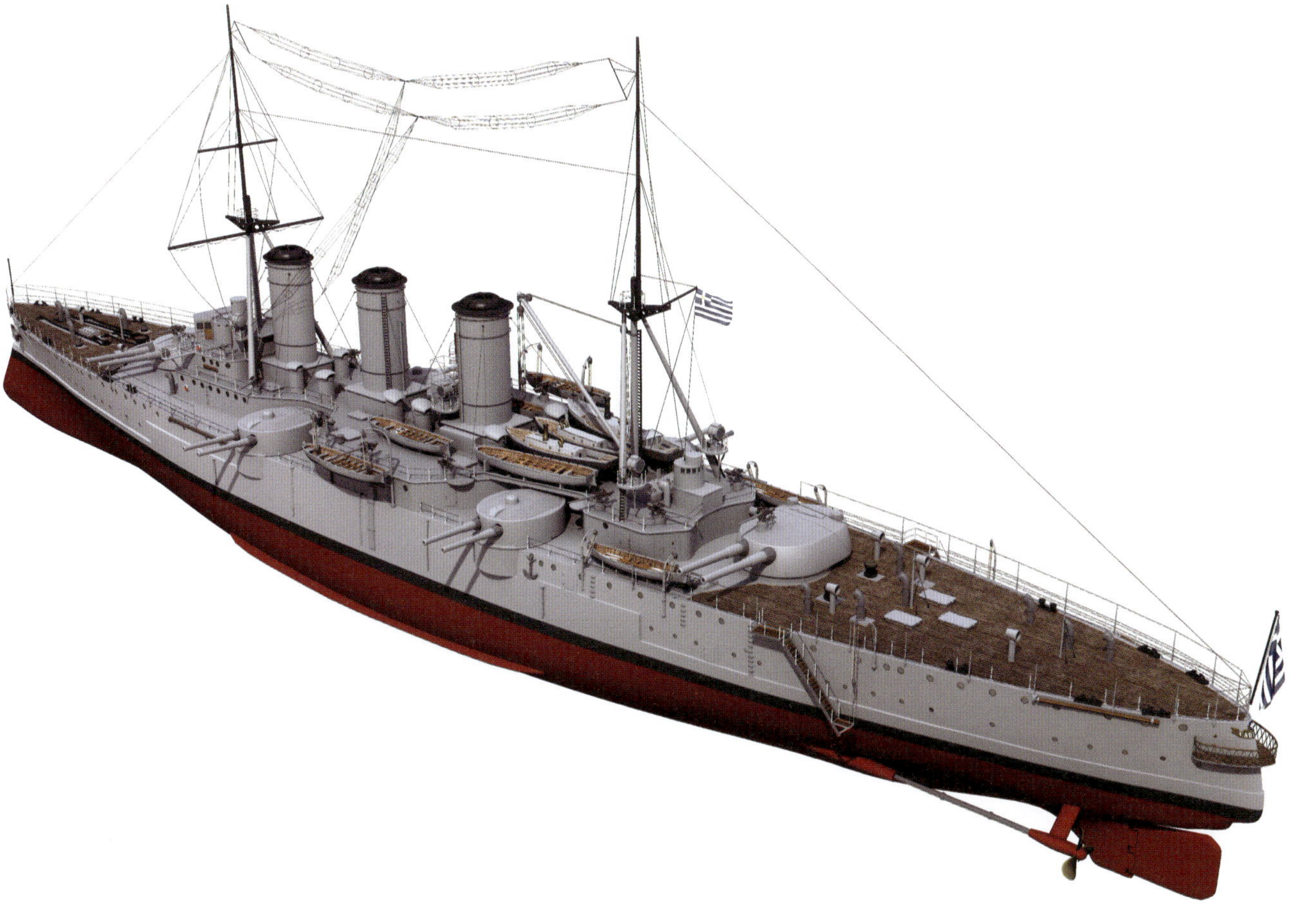

NAVAL ARCHIVES

Inside you will find:

INTERESTING ARTICLES

ARCHIVAL PHOTOS

DRAWINGS

3D ILLUSTRATIONS
AND DRAWINGS OF
THE FAMOUS WARSHIPS

ANAGLYPH 3D

Visit our shop online **shop.kagero.pl**

The Greek Armored Cruiser Georgios Averof 1911-1913 – Tassos Katsikas
LUBLIN 2018 • ISBN 978-83-65437-98-3

3D illustrations and captions, text: **Tassos Katsikas** • Design: **KAGERO STUDIO** – Łukasz Maj
KAGERO Publishing • www.kagero.pl, e-mail: kagero@kagero.pl, marketing@kagero.pl
Editorial office, Marketing, Distribution: KAGERO Publishing, Akacjowa 100, os. Borek, Turka, 20-258 Lublin 62, Poland, phone/fax (+48) 81 501 21 05
w w w . k a g e r o . e u

3D visualisations are based on the available photographs, drawings and other archive data, and should be treated only as author's attempt to recreate the original look of the particular machine as faithfully as possible. If you are in possession of materials to which author did not reach, and you would like to help us to develop a better publication, please contact the Publisher on: redakcja@kagero.pl